Access Denied!

Access Denied!

ROBERT THADD GARDNER JR.

To order additional copies of this book, contact:
Xlibris Corporation
1-888-795-4274
www.Xlibris.com
Orders@Xlibris.com
96159

Contents

The agony of defeat is felt by this father. He has not been treated fairly in Family Court. Fights with his ex-mate about spending time with his child and the lack of support from Family Court have taken a toll on this father. All he can think about is the time he has spent with his child before his access was denied.

This father is frustrated by the difficultly he has continuously experienced while trying to seek justice in Family Court. He just received another disappointing Court Order that does not do anything to stop his ex-mate from interfering with his parenting time. Yet, he refuses to give up on his never ending battle to gain access to equal justice in Family Court.

On the other side of that door, fathers find that there is an enormous amount of support in Family Court for their ex-mates.

Court Officers

Strong legal support for false reports

A father is incarcerated for his inability to pay child support. Unfortunately, he is unemployed.

Mean spirited and biased judges

Biased court appointed Parenting Coordinators

Preface

On the evening of January 9, 2010, my daughter told me her mother put soap in her mouth and spanked her. In addition, my daughter informed me of some other incidents regarding the way her mother has punished her for minor infractions. I considered the actions of my daughter's mother to be abusive and excessive.

Later that night, I filed a complaint of child abuse with the Division of Youth and Family Services (DYFS).

They responded immediately. The next day, the DYFS investigators were dispatched to visit the house where my daughter lives with her mother. The investigation into my complaint of child abuse took several days to complete. My daughter told the investigators all of the details regarding the spanking by her mother with soap in her mouth. And, my daughter informed the DYFS investigators about how her mother punishes her by making her sleep in the coldest and darkest room on the ground floor of their house. However, in the end, DYFS took the position that there were no black and blue marks detected on my daughter's body. Therefore, DYFS determined that no child abuse had occurred in this case.

In retaliation to the complaint of child abuse that I filed against my daughter's mother, she did not let me see my daughter for five consecutive months (January 2010-May 2010). During that period of time, in March of 2010, I filed a Motion in family court to enforce my parenting rights. We argued in court for approximately three months regarding this issue.

In June of 2010, the presiding judge in this case informed me that he was not going to enforce my overnight parenting rights. Instead, without any just cause, the judge reduced my previously legally established parenting time from every other weekend (Friday-Sunday) to every other Saturday (12:00pm-8:00pm). I realized then that my access to my daughter and justice in family court would forever more be denied.

Acknowledgments

I would like to thank both of my parents for the love and care they gave me as a child. Even though their marriage ended in divorce, my parents did not allow their personal feelings to interfere with their plans regarding the parenting time I spent with my father.

I thank my mother for not using me as a pawn of weaponry against my father. I believe my mother, who is now deceased, understood that I needed to have a relationship with my father. I thank my father for staking his claim on my life by spending as much time with me as he did when I was a child.

I would like to say thank you very much to my beautiful and wonderful wife, Valerie, for the wonderful marriage we have together. Your love, your kindness, your support, your understanding, your ability and willingness to communicate during times when we disagree make our marriage a wonderful source of matrimonial bliss.

Valerie, I may not say it enough, but now it will be etched in stone forever—I love you with all my heart, body, and soul! And, you are a wonderful mother to our baby boy, Isaiah.

I would be totally remiss in my duties if I did not acknowledge the work and contributions to this book by my good friend and colleague, Dr. Kenneth B. Ballard. It is because of him that I have been inspired to become a social worker and develop programs to educate people regarding the importance of having good emotional health.

Finally, kudos to any and all parents who can put aside their differences for the betterment and development of the children they have together. In these critical situations, it should never be about the adults; it should always be about what is best for the children.

Letter to my Daughter

Dear Taylor,

I am not sure if you will ever see this letter. Yet my hope is that one day you will. And when you do, please understand that all my life I have wanted to get married, have children, and raise my children. I never liked the idea of not being in the same house with my children. I always wanted to be a full-time father, and I missed that wonderful opportunity to be your dad on a full-time basis.

Unfortunately for me, and I really do believe for you too, I made a very bad choice when I married your mother. I saw early on in my relationship with her that she had issues with communication and anger. I ignored her behavior, and I married her anyway. I really hoped, at that time, things about her behavior would change for the better. But that did not happen because our lives did not improve with marriage. As a matter of fact, things got worse after we were married.

Subsequently, the choice I made to marry your mother resulted in a broken home for us. This was inevitable in that while I was married to your mother, her behavior led to lots of tension and bad relations between us, which rapidly deteriorated the bond of our marriage. Subsequently, I had no choice but to divorce her, as she abused me both physically and emotionally throughout our time together.

Since I parted ways with your mother, she has made it her quest to harass me, menace me, and make sure that she disrupts my life financially and emotionally. In addition, she has worked hard to keep you away from me.

Although it has been a very tough struggle, some good things have happened for me. This experience with your mother and the family court system has inspired me to write two relationship books to help people avoid making the same mistakes that I made in my relationship choices. My biggest hope now is that you do not tolerate insecure and mean-spirited people.

Many times, I wanted to give up on my fight for you with your mother. That is because your mother caused so much trouble that it made me sick physically, emotionally, and financially. Your mother did things that could have ended my relationship with Ms. Valerie. But our love for each other proved to be too strong for anything that your mother tried do to in her endeavor to destroy our relationship. In addition, all of my family and friends told me not to give up my fight for you. They would always say, one day, Taylor will see what her mother is doing, and she will rebel against her mother.

I hope that you do not rebel against your mother. I also hope that there will come a time that we can spend more time together without a fight with your mother. I do believe that day will come.

You should know that the issues between me and your mother are not your fault. She and I have fought about our own selfish needs and wants, none of which can be blamed on you. I love you with all of my heart, and I wish that I could have been at all of your school plays, sporting events, and other activities. But, the information regarding those events was kept away from me. Hopefully, we will make up for our lost time together in your childhood by spending more time together in your adulthood.

You are a wonderful child to have as a daughter. You have brought so many terrific parental experiences to my life. And thus far, you have exceeded my expectations of what life would be like to be your father. Always remember that "The greatest love of all is to love yourself."

With that in mind, please do not make bad decisions in your relationship choices. It is very important for you to always remember, love is an action not a word, and love is not supposed to hurt!

With all of the love in my heart,

Daddy Robert

A letter to your Ex-Mate

When you read this letter, I hope it prompts you to make a change for the better with the way you deal with me as it relates to our children.

As a father, I can make a significant contribution to the social and emotional development of our children. In this unstable world that we live in today, our children would benefit significantly from their time spent with both parents. Do not deprive our children of that opportunity because you are mad at me.

Since you are the type of parent that will be discussed in this book, you will see that these issues are much bigger than your selfish need to hurt me. You should be advised that the idea of denying me access to the children may affect our children in ways that you cannot imagine.

Years ago, the psychological impact on our children who were used as pawns did not receive much attention. However, today, using our children as pawns has expanded to psychological terms known as Parental Alienation Syndrone (PAS) and the Stockholm Syndrome.

I recently read that the long-term effects of using children as pawns include but are not limited to depression, suicide, anxiety, guilt, withdrawal from school, and social settings. In addition, some children experience feelings of shame, and symptoms of Post Traumatic Stress Disorder (PTSD).

I would like you to take some time to think about your actions. When you do things to hurt me by not letting me spend time with our children, do you realize that our children also become victims of your vindictive behavior? The effects of this type of action on our children are noted above. Hopefully, you can see that those issues are very serious as it relates to the emotional health of our children. Do you want our children to be victims or victors? As an adult, I already understand that life can be tough. But, I have to keep it moving. I have to work, pay bills, care for my new family, and live my own life.

In doing what you do to hurt me, do you really have control of the things that are important in your life? When you hurt me, do you have control of your job security? Do you have control of your credit card spending? Do you have control of the results of your next blood test? Do you have control of the life threatening diagnosis you may have just received from your doctor? Sometimes when a person focuses so much on another person, they may lose control of the things that are important regarding their own well being.

So hurt me if you must by keeping the children away from me. But know that you are also hurting yourself. And above all, please do not forget about how you may damage our children emotionally and socially because you kept them away from me. We only live once.

Our children will have only one chance to grow up. Why not let me help you give our children the best chance at living a life filled with good emotional health? Good emotional health consists of high self-esteem, good self-awareness, and lots of self-love. These are the ingredients that will give our children the best chance they can have to deal effectively in a world filled with treacherous people.

When propelled by good emotional health, our children will have a much better chance to become happy and emotionally healthy productive members of society.

Respectfully,

The father of your children!

What is Love?

What do we know about love? That is a question that could generate so many different answers from many different people. In general, when we engage intimately with another individual, we usually look for love from that person. But what are we really getting?

In your relationship endeavors, you may meet a person who knows how to love you in a way that makes you feel good. In a perfect world, it would be ideal to fall in love with someone who treats you with kindness, love and respect. In addition, when you have good communication between two people, those qualities may result in a very fulfilling relationship. For me, that would be the type of love that I would strive for in my relationships.

In other cases, we may find ourselves intimately involved with men and women who may subject us to physical abuse. In these cases, physical violence dictates the flow of those relationships. Statistics show that many people stay in abusive relationships for a variety of reasons. Although abusive behavior does not make the abused person feel good, but in the mind of the abuser, their abusive acts are done in the name of love.

Then there are others who say they love you. While at the same time, they cheat on you by loving another person. When you catch them in the act of cheating, the first thing they say is, "Baby, you know I love you."

As you can see, the idea of love can be a very confusing subject. So then, how do we really define love? Below, I have three perspectives regarding the definition of love.

The first perspective of love is defined by the King James Version of the Bible.

The second perspective of love is defined by *Webster's Ninth New Collegiate Dictionary.*

And the third perspective regarding the definition of love is defined by me as an author and your relationship expert.

The Bible says in Corinthians 1-13:1, "Love is patient, love is kind. It does not envy, it does not boast, it is not proud. It is not rude, it is not self-seeking, it is not easily angered, it keeps no record of wrongs. Love does not delight in evil but rejoices with the truth. It always protects, always trusts, always hopes, it always perseveres. Love never fails . . ."

Webster's Ninth New Collegiate Dictionary defines *love* in pertinent part, "1. to hold dear; to cherish; 2. to feel a lover's passion, devotion or tenderness; 3. to take pleasure in . . . unselfish loyal and benevolent concern for the good of another."

As for me, I believe that love is defined by some very consistent themes, which are compatible with the Bible and the dictionary.

First, I believe that love is an action, not a word. That means two people demonstrate their love for one another by doing loving things, which result in pleasurable experiences. When and if your mate mistreats you, their foul behavior should not be excused because he/she says that they love you.

Finally, I believe that love is not supposed to hurt. If your mate abuses you—physically emotionally, financially—you do not have love; you have pain. Love is a behavior that should stimulate good feelings, good times, and overall, a life filled with good experiences between two people.

I would suggest that you consider dealing with a mate whose behavior is more consistent with demonstrating loving tendencies. Let that be your guide for love in your relationship endeavors. Trying to decipher what love is can be a very confusing chain of events. But be clear. I stress to you that love should feel good. I hope you will choose that philosophy as you negotiate your relationship experiences.

If you can see what love is really supposed to be, my hope is that this is what you will strive for in your relationships. And when you are faced with anything contrary to loving experiences, you must find your way out of those relationships. If not, things may only get worse for you. You were not born to be mistreated.

That is not what God has in store for you. You are entitled to a life of love, prosperity, and happiness. And if you believe it, you can achieve it.

I would like to make one final point regarding this very important subject of love. In order to really be free to love another, you must first learn to love yourself. When you love yourself, that is the only way you can truly love someone else.

To love yourself is to feel good about who you are. When you feel good about yourself, it is a natural reaction to feel good and be good to someone else. To love yourself may improve your chances to attract people into your life who feel good about themselves.

Therefore, whether you are short, tall, fat, or small, you were born with a special God-given talent to make your mark on the world. Find out what your gift from God is so that you can be what you were born to be. Do not be discouraged. Always be encouraged. Learn to love yourself, and make a good life for you.

Part of this book is about people who have suffered as a result of the mistakes they made in choosing people to love. Those bad choices have resulted in some enormous consequences, which are described in this book. It is my hope that you are able to avoid some of these painful life experiences.

One of the ways to avoid bad relationship experiences is learn to love yourself and know what love is supposed to be.

Introduction

In this book, you will learn about the unbelievable challenges and life experiences for fathers who are denied access to their children. Quite often, when relationships between two parents end on bad terms, fathers may have to deal with angry mothers who hold their children hostage. These mothers use the children in nefarious ways to wreak havoc in the lives of good fathers.

Men who simply just want to be good fathers find themselves in confusing struggles with their children who have been brainwashed by their mothers to dislike their fathers. When fathers seek to enforce their parental rights in the very expensive, dysfunctional, and biased family court system, their hopes for justice are often denied and fall by the wayside. The judges favorable decisions are frequently awarded to mothers who violate their court orders, and are allowed to perpetuate their campaigns to keep children away from their fathers. What I have stated here only scratches the surface regarding the myriad of complicated issues that arise for fathers when their access is denied to their children.

This book also seeks to educate you about the harsh realities of life for children when they are used as pawns by their angry mothers, and in some cases, fathers are guilty of this behavior, as well. This game, which is played by parents when they use their children as pawns is what I refer to throughout this book as "Child Pawn." In the game of child pawn, one parent uses the children as a weapon to hurt the other parent. This act is usually carried out by the mother who, in most cases, is awarded custodial parental rights under family law to be the primary care taker of the children after a divorce.

On the surface, child pawn may sound harmless. But, in reality, child pawn can have a devastating effect on the emotional health and social development of your children. Unfortunately, if your relationship with a mate ends on bad terms, the intricacies, difficulties, and challenges related to child pawn can affect you and your children in a negative fashion that may last for years.

There are many fathers, which include me, who pursue justice regarding issues related to their children who are victims of child pawn. However, as noted above, there are so many of us who do not receive justice from the family court legal system. Instead, we receive arbitrary and capricious decisions from biased judges who operate in a tyrannical fashion throughout the United States.

I experienced firsthand the heartbreaking feeling of having my daughter turned against me by her mother. I also witnessed the guilt and confusion experienced by my daughter when she was forced by her mother to tell me that she did not want to spend any time with me. As a result of this type of parental warfare, our innocent children are emotionally damaged at home, at school, at the playground, and at the baby sitters house. Internally, these children are depressed, confused, and filled with guilt when they are told by one parent to hurt and disrupt the life of their other parent.

Unfortunately for me and many other fathers, we have not had adequate support from family court in our legal battles to resolve these issues. Our efforts could be helped tremendously in a more balanced and open minded family court system. Throughout this book I also point out how fathers tend to not have any leverage in family court, which is the only place available for fathers to address the ills of access denied and child pawn. Consequently, in family court, some judges totally ignore the importance of fathers in the lives of their children. The rights of fathers are ignored and significantly diminished.

Therefore, I would like to proclaim, in this book, that fathers do make a difference in the lives of their children. Fathers are much more than a child support vending machine. And there is a very important intangible element of fatherhood that is totally ignored by the family court system. When little boys grow up to be violent criminals, the administrators of correctional systems attribute their behavior to the absence of a father in their lives when they were children.

When it comes to little girls, they often seem to have a special affection for their fathers. That is what we usually call a "Daddy's Girl." When little girls turn out to be pregnant teenage mothers with low self esteem, social workers usually attribute their behavior to the absence of a father in the lives of these emancipated teenagers. The fact of the matter is that little boys and little girls need their fathers. Essentially, when the father is not present, the bad behavior of boys and girls is often associated with the absence of the father.

Parenting is a joint venture whether the parents are together in the same household or not. It takes two people to make a baby, and it would certainly benefit your children immensely if they have active relationships with both parents before and after the break up of their family. Perhaps one day the family court system will place a much higher value on the importance of fathers in the lives of their children.

Thank you very much for selecting this book to read. I assure you that you will enjoy this reading experience. To enhance key learning points in this book, you will see small icons. These icons have been inserted throughout this book to point out important information that could help you deal more effectively with issues related to access denied.

On the next page, you will see examples of these icons and the definitions regarding each icon.

This icon is a symbol that represents letting go of bad memories, bad experiences, and bad people.

This icon alerts you to good ideas to improve your quality of life.

This icon says do not even think about considering any options related to a subject where this icon appears in this book.

This icon alerts you to pay attention to specific information regarding a particular issue noted in this book.

This icon cautions you to consider the consequences of your decisions related to an issue where this icon appears in this book.

Terms and Phrases to Know

As you read this book, you will come across a myriad of terms and phrases. Particularly in chapter 3, "Evidence of Access Denied," you will find the majority of these terms. These terms and phrases are defined in detailed below. I hope by providing these definitions for you that it will make for a more user-friendly reading experience.

Terms/Acrynoms	Definitions
Arbitrator	Neutral third party in labor disputes
ADHD	Attention Deficit Hyperactive Disorder
Ex-Mate	A reference to a former significant other
DYFS	Division of Youth and Family Services-New Jersey Child Welfare Agency-Investigates cases of abuse and neglect regarding children
Motion	An application made to a court for the purpose of obtaining an order directing some act to be done in favor of the applicant
Notice of Cross Motion	A formal written notice presented in court by a defendant in response to a claim presented by a plaintiff
Notice of Motion for Reconsideration	A formal written request to a judge to rescind his/her court order

Court Order	A written decision from a judge regarding issues presented in a Motion; a judge decides for or against the relief you seek in your Motion
Plaintiff	A person who brings a court action by filing a Motion; a person who seeks relief for injury to their rights
Defendant	The person of whom recovery or relief is sought in a court action; the accused in a criminal case
Pro Se	A person who does not retain a lawyer; a person represents himself/herself in court
Evidence	Materials offered to prove the existence or non-existance of a fact
Parties	The opposing people or groups involved in a legal action
Law Clerk	A law school graduate who serves as a personal assistant to the judge

Angry Female
Ex-Mate

Please note, what I say in this chapter is in no way shape or fashion intended to be a bashing of women.

I do recognize the fact that there are good, loving mothers who do not use their children as pawns. Therefore, in this chapter, please understand I may be talking to you or I may be talking about you.

If I am talking about you, I do not mean to offend you. Instead, I hope to impart some knowledge regarding the emotional damage you may cause when you participate in acts of "Child Pawn." As noted throughout this text, the indirect effect of this game on your children can have a devastating impact on their emotional and social development.

On the other hand, if I am talking to you, I hope not only to educate you, but also I hope to discourage you from ever participating in the game of child pawn. As you know, this game is intended to hurt the father of your children. However, the real pain of your game is felt by your children instead.

If you really love your children, do not sacrifice their happiness for your anger. This is a game that nobody wins. You may enjoy pleasures of the moment while you seek to hurt your ex-mate. However, your children may experience emotional turmoil for the rest of their lives.

If you are a disgruntled ex-mate, are you aware of how important it is for your children to have good emotional health? Do you know what elements contribute to having good emotional health? For the record, please be advised that emotional health pertains to the internal strength of your children. It has to do with their self-esteem, self-love, self-awareness and their ability to forgive others. If these elements are functioning at a high level within your children, that may result in your children having a more positive outlook on life. And, it will help them feel much better about who they are as individuals.

The synergy of all of the aforementioned elements working together will certainly boost the self-confidence of your children. Without good emotional health, your children may look for satisfaction and love in all the wrong places. With good emotional health your child may be more inclined to living a more fulfilled life and better equipped to accomplish their goals.

Good emotional health could lead to more successful endeavors in their lives regarding choices, careers, relationships, and their interpersonal skills. As a disgruntled parent, you may severely jeopardize your children's chances to develop good emotional health.

Essentially, the way you behave when you set out to hurt your ex-mate is a prime example of the behavior of a person who has bad emotional health. Such behavior clearly demonstrates your inability to be emotionally strong and let go of past relationships. Is this the example you want to set for your children? Our children watch what we do. They emulate our behavior. If they see us communicate through violent, vindictive, and noncommunicative ways, our children may behave that way in similar situations.

I have seen the effect we, as parents, have on our children. Our behavior can transfer to our children like electricity in wires. It is important to recognize that what you do to your ex-mate is much bigger than you. More specifically, our children tend to adopt the same methods for resolving their issues, which they inherit from us.

For instance, as a child, I spent time visiting many of my relatives. Although I enjoyed the time I shared with my family, there were times that some of my visits were ruined. This had to do with the way one of my family members treated his wife. He was verbally abusive toward her. He would yell and scream at her when she voiced her opinion.

I felt her pain. I shared in the embarrassment and disrespect she experienced during those times. I could not understand why my aunt was verbally abused by her husband.

Now, let's fast-forward 20 years later. I saw another relative mistreat his wife. He is the son of the person I described above. Over the years, I have witnessed him mistreat his wife the same way his father verbally abused his mother.

He disrespects his wife in and out of their house. There is one incident that comes to mind I will never forget. One day, my relative's wife and I watched our children play together. His child accidently tripped and fell.

As his wife and I were encouraging his son to get up off the ground, my relative stuck his head out of his bedroom window. He reacted to hearing us tell his child to get up.

Suddenly, he screamed at his wife, "You pick my son up off the ground and bring him in this house right now!"

Here again, I was embarrassed for his wife too. The behavior of my relative was unprovoked, unwarranted, and totally unnecessary. It was apparent to me that this relative learned to verbally abuse his wife by what he observed when he saw his father verbally abuse his mother.

As you can see, my uncle and his son have the same behavior as it relates to their spouses. This is a clear case of "like father, like son." The bad fruit did not fall far from the tree.

In another scenario and a much lighter situation, I saw the direct effect of how a father's behavior had a direct impact on his daughter. This scenario was funny to me, but it was not a laughing matter.

One day I was riding the Number 2 train into Manhattan from the Bronx. While on the train, I sat across from a man who was eating chicken wings. He shared his chicken wings with his daughter. Every time the train stopped and the doors opened, from his seat, the man threw his chicken bones onto the floor of the subway platform.

At one stop, when the train doors opened, the man's daughter threw her chicken bones onto the floor of the subway platform. When the little girl's father saw what she did, he yelled at her and said, "Why did you throw those chicken bones out of the train? You are supposed to put the bones in the garbage!"

I was shocked to see the father handle his daughter in that way. After all, he had been throwing chicken bones out of the train every time it stopped, and the doors opened.

When the man finished yelling at his daughter, she said, "Daddy, I am doing what you do."

Her father yelled back at her, "You don't do what I do!"

Here, you have a parent who set a bad example for his daughter. Then he berated her for the bad behavior she learned from him. Are you the kind of parent that would not want your child to do what you do? If so, be mindful that you have to lead by setting good examples for your children. As parents, most of us want our children to enjoy better lives than we had. Are you that type of parent? If the answer is yes, then you may have to change your behavior. Remember, the good life we want for our children starts with us as parents.

Therefore, you must focus on the emotional needs of your children after the breakup of your relationship with the other parent. He may be gone forever, but the children are left behind for you to nurture into becoming productive members of society. To promote a better quality of life for your children, direct your attention to raising their self-esteem, increasing their self-awareness, and teaching them how to love themselves.

If you find ways to strengthen the emotional health of your children, it will enhance their chances of feeling good and being happy with who they are. This is vital to their chances of finding happy and healthy relationships with themselves and others.

What does it mean to have children who have good emotional health? Are you familiar with the saying, "Only the strong survive?"

When I say strong, I am not talking about a body filled with muscles. A muscle-bound body does not give a person the strength to handle very challenging and highly stressful situations like (death, sudden breakups and unemployment). Muscles may only help you to look good on the outside. Good emotional health will help your children to be strong on the inside. That way, they are better equipped to handle the many trials and tribulations they will experience in their lifetime.

Most people are not even aware of the significance of having good emotional health. It is a very important topic as it relates to how we feel inside. Good emotional health is what makes happy people thrive on feeling good about the life they live. And bad emotional health is what makes people look down, feel bad about themselves and fail to live life to the fullest. Bad emotional health is what makes rich people commit suicide.

As long as you are in the business of hurting your ex-mate, you will also be in the business of neglecting your responsibility to nurture the emotional health of yourself and your children. What is more important to you?

Further, what do you really gain when you hurt someone else? If your children suffer in the process, then everybody loses.

In addition, have you ever dared to take a look at the astronomical multifaceted cost of your vindictive behavior?

First, the cost of your behavior comes at the expense of a better quality of life for you and your children. Second, there is an adverse impact on your own financial resources, as it relates to the attorney's fees you pay. Third, you lose time from work. In addition, you increase your chances to decrease your own quality time at home. It is simply a no-win situation for everyone involved.

Finally, I discovered something good about the sad experiences I had when my ex-wife denied my access to my daughter. Did you know your actions to deny access to the children may create opportunities for your ex-mate? It is very simple.

If your ex-mate had more time to spend with the children, he may not have time to improve the quality of his life. But, if you interfere with his parenting time, that will create opportunities for him to make strides to change his life for the better. The extra time will facilitate his ability to work on some of his own dreams.

On the next few pages, take a look at the many positive things that happened for me while my access to my daughter was denied. Some of these things were accomplished during my marriage and after my divorce.

My Gains through Pain

Life can be painfully challenging when you are denied access to your children by your ex-mate. For me, it was a very confusing journey filled with sadness, madness, and little hope for happiness. Eventually, I realized I had to find a light at the end of the tunnel. I knew it would be up to me to open my eyes so I could see that light. I had limited options to choose from.

The first option would be for me to remain brokenhearted. The second option would be to find a better way to handle this very tough situation. Subsequently, I began to see the lack of time spent with my daughter as an opportunity to do some things to improve the quality of my life. I found that to be the best way to handle this very tough situation.

I stated earlier that everybody loses in these dysfunctional post relationship situations. However, there are times when the ex-mate you seek to hurt can gain from the things you take away. Sometimes this person may take advantage of the free time you created for them when you denied access to their children.

I would like to state from my own experience that the pain you cause your ex-mate can turn into gains for your ex-mate. That person can experience happiness and success when you keep the children away from him. Take a look at some of my "Gains through Pain" which are outlined below.

1. When my daughter was an infant, her mother tended to her needs when she cried in the middle of the night. I never heard my daughter cry because I sleep very hard. Instead of waking me up to help, my ex-wife took care of our daughter during those times.
2. Then, my ex-wife would insist that she needed a break from our daughter. She demanded that I take care of our daughter every weekend.
3. My daughter's mother saw this as a way to punish me. She believed I would see this as women's work. She was wrong. During the three years I lived with my daughter and her mother, I spent every weekend with my daughter. As a result of the love and care I gave my daughter, we bonded in a way her mother now envies.
4. In January 2010, my ex-wife interfered with my parenting time for approximately six months. Due to the additional time she created for me by not allowing me to spend time with my daughter, I completed the writing of my first book, *The Choices We Make.* I was also inspired to create an online T-shirt store.

5. With my T-shirts, I promote my ideas for healthy relationships, which are described in my book. To learn more about my first book and my online T-shirt store, please see my website: rtgardnerjr.com.
6. In the spring of 2010, I organized a public speaking campaign. In this campaign, I reach out to schools, churches, and other community organizations to educate people regarding my ideas for healthy relationships.
7. In June 2010, a family court judge reduced my parenting time to one day (Saturday) every other weekend. The additional free time allowed me to write my second book, *Access Denied*, which is the book you are reading now.
8. In the fall of 2010, I decided that I would like to counsel and educate people on a professional level regarding the importance of having good emotional health. I applied to graduate school.
9. I was accepted to study for a master's degree in social work. Now I believe that the sky is the limit for me. I will continue to turn my life around and not be overwhelmed by the evil deeds of my ex-mate.

Overall, I will admit the pain of not spending time with my daughter hurts very much. Now I understand my parenting time has been diminished by people I cannot control. I have turned my lemons into lemonade. I will continue to stay productive. I decided to take my life back thanks to my ex-wife.

If you are a person who uses your children as pawns, I hope by now you see that is a no-win situation for all involved. In some cases, your ex-mate may actually benefit from your game of child pawn. Think about it. Is it really worth it to you?

You may cause some heartache in the life of your ex-mate. But if you do the math, you will see how you hurt yourself and your children financially, emotionally, and spiritually in the process. Hopefully, I have helped you to think about a better way to handle your business regarding your children with your ex-mate.

Learn to let go of bad relationships, bad memories, and all those people who have not been good to you. Holding onto bad experiences only increases your pain. Letting go will help you to heal. When you let go of yesterday, you can make room for tomorrow and receive the blessings that follow!

My Access Denied

In June 2004, my divorce from my abusive ex-wife was finalized. Shortly thereafter, I began to have experiences that indicated my access would be denied to some basic fundamental things in life. For instance, I had no peace of mind. I had to fight with my ex-wife to see my daughter. A major part of my income was tied up in postmarital legal affairs.

Due to my very limited financial resources, I struggled mightily to pay my bills. I could not save any money. And I could not afford to buy a sufficient amount of food to eat on a daily basis.

It was very stressful for me when I had to deal with issues regarding my ex-wife. I could not talk about her to another person unless I yelled and screamed as I described my experiences with her. After my first marriage ended, my freedom came with a very expensive and stressful price tag.

In the literal sense, access denied sounds like being physically denied access into a building or a restricted area on a military base. However, in this text, I am talking about a feeling and experience of my access being denied to a good quality of life. This would include a lack of equal justice in family court.

Although the signs were evident that my access to a good quality of life was diminishing rapidly, I did not fully understand how the aforementioned experiences could be attributed to the subject of access denied. It was not until I started looking back at all the limitations on my life, which for the most part, were related to my legal fees and the exorbitant amount of child support I was required to pay at that time. For the record, I do believe in providing financial support for my children. However, the New Jersey Child Support Guidelines are constructed in a way that precludes the obligator from being able to afford anything else.

According to the New Jersey Child Support Guidelines, it was determined that my biweekly child support obligation would be $440, or $880 per month. This was based on my annual salary of $80,000 and the annual salary of my ex-wife. At the time of our divorce, she earned $110,000 per year. In addition, she earned a five-figure annual salary bonus, as well.

I felt the initial shock of what my child support obligation did to my disposable income. But I had no idea regarding the full extent of the damage that would be done to my life overall. I was totally unaware of how child support would deny my access to some very basic things like food, carfare, dry cleaning, toiletries, and gas. Now, as I have had a chance to assess my life during those times, it is clear that my experience with this matter has been appropriately named "Access Denied."

There is a very important lesson related to my struggle during those times. The lesson for you would be that no matter how difficult things are for you in the midst of a tough life experience, do not ever give up. Although these challenges may seem like they consume all your time and thoughts, which they did to me. However, not for one minute did I think about giving up on myself or my life. You must stay positive and keep striving to live the life you want to live. My life is evidence that you too will get pass your toughest time in life. You know what they say, "If tough times do not kill you, they will make you stronger."

As time went on, I became somewhat accustomed to the limitations on my life due to my child support obligation and the battles in and out of court with my daughter's mother. I had experienced some major setbacks in family court.

My experience with access denied to equal justice was beginning to manifest itself in family court. For instance, there had been several instances where my daughter's mother had violated our divorce settlement agreement. I took her to court every time she violated that agreement. However, I did not receive any favorable decisions from any of the judges to enforce my rights. Through it all, I kept living and I just went with the flow. Then, on January 30, 2010, I had an explosive revelation that led to my access being denied to my daughter in a way I would have never imagined.

On this day, I eagerly made my way to my daughter's basketball game. The one-hour drive seemed like it took forever. When I arrived at the Recreation Center, it was crowded and the game was in progress. It was very entertaining to watch these little girls play basketball.

After the game, my daughter stopped to speak to her mother for a minute. Then she ran over and thanked me for coming to her game. I told her it was my pleasure to be there. I asked her to change into her clothes so we could do the things I had planned for the day.

My daughter looked at me and said, "Daddy, I do not want to do an overnight with you at your house this weekend."

I told her I am aware of that, but I thought we would spend the day together.

Then my daughter said, "Daddy, I do not want to be with you this weekend."

I said, "Taylor, what are you talking about? What do you mean that you do not want to be with me this weekend?"

She said, "I just don't."

I said, "Taylor, let me talk to you for a minute. I would like to know what is going on here."

I pulled my daughter to the side so we could talk. Less than two minutes later her mother came to where we were sitting in the gym.

Her mother said, "Your time is up. I am leaving to go to the hospital."

I told her to just run along, and I will bring Taylor to her later that evening.

Her mother said, "That is not going to happen. She does not want to go with you."

I said, "That is what you told her to say when I spoke to her on the telephone Thursday. I want to see what Taylor has to say about spending time with me today. So please, let me talk to Taylor for five minutes. Would you please excuse us."

Instead of her mother leaving the area, she moved closer to us. This made it difficult for me to talk to my daughter. I asked her mother again to please excuse us. Her mother refused to leave the area. I told her mother that I am not going to fight with her. I will just go to the other side of the gym.

I took my daughter by her hand to move to another area in the gymnasium. At that moment, in the middle of this gymnasium filled with people, my daughter's mother screamed, "You let her go."

I was shocked! At that moment, I realized that this woman set me up. She orchestrated a scenario in a public place to depict me as trying to illegally take my daughter from her.

I moved in real close to her. We were face to face and I said, "How dare you (the Abuser) tell me how to treat our daughter"

While I was up close in her face, she repeatedly bumped into me with her right hip in a way that nobody could see. This I believe was an act to provoke me into a physical altercation with her. I told her she was crazy to use this prank in her attempt to assassinate my character.

She then shouted to her friends in the crowd, "Call the police, call the police." At that point, all hell broke loose in the gym. The people in the crowd were shouting at me to leave her alone. Some of the men in the stands left their seats and came after me.

The moment I realized I had been set up. I should have remained calm and left the Recreation Center. However, I allowed my emotions to obfuscate my ability to think clearly in that situation. I was overcome by my desire to spend time with my daughter. At all times, you have to be smart. You must think with your head and not react based on your emotional state of mind.

These men demanded that I leave the gym. They said, "This is not a place for violence."

I yelled back at them and said, "I am only here to talk to my daughter. And I am going to talk to her. So you all need to back off."

I turned to my daughter. I took her by the hand so we could go somewhere else and talk. Her mother grabbed her other hand. We had a tug of war with our daughter. I pulled her in one direction. Her mother pulled her in another direction. Then I could feel my daughter trying to break free from my hand. Eventually, she did break free from me and she ran. I ran after her crying and begging her to tell me what was going on here. My daughter screamed, "Leave me alone."

She said, "Stop fighting with Mommy. I do not want to go with you."

I said, "Taylor, what is going on? Why are you doing this?"

Then she ran toward the crowd on the other side of the gymnasium. She was embraced by a group of women. They took my daughter out of the gym to a place where I could not see her. I was furious, confused, embarrassed, and brokenhearted all at the same time. Right before my eyes, I witnessed the work of my ex-wife as she had turned my daughter against me.

I was then escorted out of the gym by the facility manager. On my way out, I explained to him that I was not there to start any trouble. I informed him that this was my weekend to be with my daughter. However, her mother would not let her go with me. I further explained to the facility manager that I drove sixty miles to see my daughter. I had no idea her mother would not allow me to spend any time with my daughter.

I also told the facility manager that my daughter's mother is retaliating against me for reporting her to DYFS for abusing our daughter. And as part of her retaliation, she knowingly had me travel all this way. Her decision to preclude me from spending any time with our daughter was premeditated. My presence at the Recreation Center was necessary for her to carry out this plan. And she succeeded in her attempt to create a scene in the gym that would cause me to act out, as I did.

As I was about to conclude my discussion with the facility manager, I told him that this was a very strange situation for me. Three weeks ago, my daughter complained to me that her mother put a bar of soap in her mouth and beat her. And today, I came here to see how she was doing. And, I wanted to work on the healing process with my daughter regarding that experience. However, my daughter treated me as if I put the soap in her mouth and beat her.

Then, I stepped outside of the Recreation Center, and the police had just arrived. I introduced myself to the police. I told them what happened at the Recreation Center. I also made a request to the police to allow me an opportunity to speak to my daughter for five minutes. The police assured me that I would have an opportunity to speak to my daughter.

I continued my discussion with the police. I gave them more details regarding the events that took place in the Recreation Center. I informed the police that on January 9, 2010, my daughter told me her mother has been doing some very mean things to her. My daughter told me her mother punishes her by making her sleep downstairs on the ground floor of their three-story townhouse in the back room, which is cold and dark. I also told the police that my daughter informed me that she recently got into trouble at school by speaking out of turn in class. The incident was reported to her mother. When my daughter arrived home, her mother took her upstairs. My daughter said her mother opened a brand new bar of soap, put it in her mouth, and beat her. When her mother stopped beating her, the mother took the soap out of her mouth. In response to that story, I called the DYFS child abuse hot line and filed a complaint of abuse against my ex-wife. Now, my ex-wife is retaliating against me. She orchestrated an incident in the Recreation Center that almost caused a riot. In addition, she will not let me spend any time with my daughter, and it is my scheduled weekend to be with my daughter.

After I finished telling the police my story, my daughter's mother spoke to the police. Then, my daughter was brought out of hiding. As she approached me, my eyes were filled with tears. I said to my daughter "I do not know why you did what you did to me in the gym." I told her that "I loved her with all my heart."

I said to her, "I am not sure what is going on here. But you should know that I forgive you. And when you are ready, I will be happy to pick you up so we could spend some time together."

Then, I said good-bye. And when I walked away from my daughter, I started crying incessantly. I got into my car. I called my wife to tell her what happened at the Recreation Center. I told her how I was set up by my daughter's mother.

While I was telling my wife the story, I could barely talk to her, as I cried like a baby. I could not believe that my daughter turned against me, and she ran away from me.

I was stunned that my daughter broke my heart. My wife told me over and over again that my daughter was told by her mother to behave the way she did. My wife also said, "Taylor would not have done that to you unless she was forced by her mother to behave that way." My wife believed that my daughter's mother brainwashed my child. My wife told me that "Taylor had to do what her mother wanted. She lives in the house with her mother. And it is in her best interest to carry out her mother's plan, which she did by saying that she did not want to be with you." I felt somewhat relieved that my wife helped me to understand my daughter's behavior in that situation.

Full Access Granted
A good way to punish your ex-mate

In July 2010, my new wife gave birth to our baby boy. We have enjoyed our new baby immensely. However, it was during my experience as a father with my son that I discovered full access to your children can be a huge responsibility.

In July 2011, my wife went away for three weeks on a business trip. I was the sole care taker of our son. On the first day, my son got sick. I spent the entire day trying to figure our what was wrong with him. He would not eat and he cried all day long. I did not find out until much later that day that he might have an ear infection. A friend of the family told me his symptoms seemed to be similar to her experience with her children. I went to a number of stores later that night to purchase various medications to ease his pain. I had to read many labels. I had to choose from a wide variety of children's medications to make sure I purchased a safe product for my son.

On day two, there was no improvement in his condition. I called my son's doctor to request an emergency appointment. Then, I had to get him dressed and I rushed him to the doctor's office. The doctor diagnosed his illness as an ear infection. After the appointment with the doctor, I had to run to the pharmacist to get his prescriptions filled.

Throughout the first three days with my son he did not eat well. He cried a lot because he was sick. And, he did not sleep well at night. By the end of day three, the medications began to take effect, and his condition improved. Then, for the next 16 days I could not move around the house to take care of chores and personal business. My son wanted me to carry him everywhere I went in the house. When I put him down he cried. Then he followed me all over the house, and even into the bathroom. At night, he would not go to sleep unless I laid down with him. When he did sleep at night, he would not sleep through the night. I was awakened by the sound of his crying, his cooing, and him slapping me in the face after he climbed out of his crib into my bed. I was shocked to find him in my bed. That changed my state of mind from being totally incoherent to being wide awake in the middle of the night.

During the times he woke up in the middle of the night, I had to change his pampers and feed him. Afterwards, I had to put him back to sleep either by putting him in the bed with me or lying on the floor and rocking him to sleep. My son defecated and urinated a lot everyday. Bathing him and ironing his clothes was easy compared to the amount of soiled pampers I had to change. In addition, he had to eat every two hours. This required me to make bottles, clean bottles, and sing lots of songs to stop my son from crying, if I was late giving him his bottle.

I love being a parent. But, I never had the full responsibility to care for either one of my two children. Through this experience, I developed a new found love and respect for single mothers. Personally, I do not know how you all function as a single parent.

I do believe that if you are angry with your ex-mate, and you want to punish him for ending his relationship with you, then insist that he spend time with your children. That would be the best way to get back at your ex-mate for breaking up with you. In addition, the children would benefit immensely from the time spent with both parents. Further, ensuring that your ex-mate spends time with your children will give you a much needed break.

Based on the time I spent with my son, I know for sure that as a single parent you will need a break. We love our children. Nevertheless, parenting is a tremendous responsibility. Anybody who intentionally makes themself a single parent by not allowing the other parent to spend time with the children is totally insane. If you really want to hurt your ex-mate, take him to court and insist that a judge give you a court order that demands he spends time with your children. The best way to use your children as pawns is to give them to their father. Then you can be free to do what you want to do every other weekend. Yes, do you!

You do the math. If you keep the children away from their father, in the beginning that may hurt his feelings and maybe even break his heart. Subsequently, his phone will begin to ring. His imagination will begin to flow. Before you know it, he will be out gallivanting around town enjoying all of the free time you gave him because you did not let him spend time with his children.

On the other hand, if your children's father is required to spend time with the kids, he has to spend money in addition to the child support he has to pay. His free time will be limited, and his quality time will be spent with the children instead of his new girlfriend. Me, I do not want to be a single parent. Without the revenge factor, can you think of one good reason why you would intentionally make yourself a single parent? If you can, please check into the nearest mental health facility, and admit yourself for treatment as an insane human being. Again, if you really want to punish your ex-mate for leaving you, make him spend time with his children!

Evidence of Access Denied

The next time I was scheduled to see my daughter was Friday, February 13, 2010. At that point in time, I was bursting with anxiety. I wanted to know about the climate in the house with her mother after the DYFS investigation. I was also very concerned that my daughter might be subjected to some serious subliminal sanctions by her mother. I knew that her mother would be on the war path.

On February 12, 2010, I called my daughter to confirm the time I would pick her up on Friday. When I spoke to her regarding our weekend together she said, "Daddy, I do not want to go with you this weekend. I do *not* want to go, *do not*!" Once again, I was mortified, surprised and totally heartbroken. As much as I believed that her mother was influencing my daughter's behavior, it was beginning to sound like my daughter really did not want to be with me. In my heart, I wanted to believe that could not be the case based on my strong relationship with my daughter and the circumstances regarding this matter. However, I was an emotional wreck. I felt disconnected from my child. I sadly responded and said, "Okay Taylor, I love you and I will talk to you again in two weeks."

My daughter's alleged refusal to spend time with me during our scheduled parenting time was very difficult for me to handle. Therefore, I decided to take her mother to court. I wanted a judge to stop her from interfering with my parenting time. I filed the legal papers to request a court date. Subsequently, our case was scheduled to be heard March 19, 2010. However, unbeknownst to me the judge rescheduled the case for another date. I went to court as scheduled on March 19, 2010. As I sat in the court room waiting for my case to be called, the judge's law clerk informed me that my case had been rescheduled. The law clerk told me that he notified the Defendant (ex-wife). He requested that she inform me of the schedule change. She did not inform me. I traveled 60 miles from my house to the court house. This was merely another act of revenge by the ex-wife to create another bad experience for me.

I expressed my disappointment to the law clerk about not being informed regarding the rescheduled court date. After all, I filed the original legal papers (Motion) to initiate this process. Yet he notified her. And, he requested that she inform me of the new court date. In the back of my mind, I knew it would not behoove me to complain too much. The law clerk works directly with the judge. So, I humbly made my feelings known to him, and I went home.

My case was rescheduled approximately ten days later to March 30, 2010. On that day, to my surprise, the Defendant (ex-wife) did not show. She did not respond to the Motion I filed to bring this matter to court. I got excited. I thought her absence was an acknowledgment, on her part, that she illegally interfered with my parenting time. Therefore, I believed that this issue would be resolved in an expeditious fashion. When the judge requested that I tell him what happen, I told the judge that I reported the defendant to DYFS. This report came after my daughter informed me that her mother put soap in her mouth and beat her. I also informed the judge that my report to DYFS included the fact that my daughter's mother punishes her excessively for minor issues. She does this by making her sleep in the darkest, coldest room on the ground floor of their house. Since I reported these incidents to DYFS, my daughter's mother has not allowed me to spend time with my daughter during my scheduled parenting time weekends.

As I continued to tell my side of the story, I reiterated to the judge that since I made the report to DYFS my daughter's mother is retaliating against me. This is evidenced by the fact that she is interfering with my parenting time. She is instructing my daughter to tell me that she does not want to spend time with me. My ex-wife is using my daughter as a pawn to cover up what she is really doing to interfere with my parenting time. I told the judge that this has been going on since January 30, 2010. And based on the amount of my lost parenting time, I requested that the judge restore my lost visits with five consecutive weekend make up dates. At the conclusion of my testimony, the judge rendered his decision. In his Court Order, the judge only awarded me one makeup date, which was scheduled for the weekend of 4/30/10-5/2/10.

In addition, the judge's court order required that my parenting time resume the weekend of 4/9/10. He verbally stated that if the defendant does not comply with his court order, he would issue a warrant for her arrest. The judge further stated that he would sanction her, as well. In conclusion, the judge instructed me to mail a copy of his Court Order to the defendant by certified mail, which I did.

At that point, I had another Court Order to strengthen my already legally established parenting time, which had been previously set forth in my original divorce Settlement Agreement. I thought this additional Court Order would be of significant help to me, since my parenting rights have been violated on numerous occasions by my ex-wife. And so, I looked forward to the resumption of my overnight parenting time.

On April 8, 2010, I called my daughter's mother to schedule the pick up time with her. However, my daughter answered the telephone. My daughter told me that she did not want to stay with me that weekend. Here again, I was taken aback by what my daughter said. I knew for sure that her mother received the judge's Court Order. I had a copy of her certified mail receipt. However, during this call, it became clear to me that my daughter's mother did not take her "Spell" off of our child. My daughter adamantly declared that I should not pick her up for the weekend. Before I hung up the phone with my daughter, her mother took the phone. The mother informed me that her attorney advised her to ignore the judge's Court Order. Consequently, I did not spend any parenting time with my daughter that weekend.

Shortly thereafter, I wrote a letter to the judge. I informed him that the Defendant (ex-wife) did not comply with his Court Order. Two weeks passed, I did not receive a response from the judge. I made another attempt to pick up my daughter two weeks later on April 23, 2010. I was met with the same resistance from both my daughter and her mother. I missed another weekend of parenting time. The next week, April 30, 2010, was supposed to be my "Make up weekend" that was awarded to me by the judge. On this weekend, my daughter's mother informed me that I could only spend the day (Saturday) with my daughter. She said I could not take my daughter back to my house for an overnight visit. I turned down that option. Instead, I filed a complaint with the local police department. Consequently, I missed out on another weekend to spend time with my daughter. I sent a second letter to the judge regarding this chain of events. I included a copy of my police report with that letter.

Yet again, two weeks went by, and I did not receive any response from the judge. Therefore, on or about May 7, 2010, I submitted court papers to file a second Motion to address the fact that my ex-wife still has not allowed me to have overnight visits with my daughter. My next court date was scheduled for May 14, 2010. Then, on or about May 12, 2010, I received a package in the mail. It was a response from my ex-wife's attorney regarding my parenting time complaint. Her attorney submitted a "Notice of Motion for Reconsideration." They were attempting to have the judge rescind his earlier decision to have my ex-wife resume my parenting time. After my review of the issues listed in this document, I was blown away by her false accusations. I could not believe the lies, the deception, the irrelevant story lines and all of her deflection away from the real issues in this case.

In her response, the defendant alleged that our daughter did not want to spend any time with me. She claimed that my daughter was afraid to be with me. In addition, the defendant made many other false claims about why my daughter did not want to spend time with me. However, she did not provide any evidence to support her false accusations. In her legal papers, there were no letters from my daughter, no letters from any school counselors, and there were no letters from any medical staff that stated that my daughter had any fears about spending time with me on the weekends.

The only issue in this case was that my daughter's mother would not let me have my overnight visits with our daughter. And, I strongly believed that she coerced our daughter to say she did not want to spend time with me. As I said earlier, this was done to cover up the fact that my ex-wife was retaliating against me by interfering with my parenting time. She sought revenge on me for filing a complaint of child abuse against her with the Division of Youth and Family Services (DYFS).

Still, the one thing that stood out the most for me after my review of her court papers is that she did not provide any evidence to support her claim. This would have been required. In her court papers she accused me of being "Aggressive, turbulent and forceful with our daughter." However, there were no written statements from my daughter regarding these false allegations. Nor, did my daughter's mother provide any written reports from either a child therapist or child advocate to support her claim that our daughter had issues with me. The bottom line is that my ex-wife was not telling the truth. This was substantiated by the fact that she had no evidence to support her false accusations.

At this point in time, several months had gone by and I have not seen my daughter. The judge did not follow through on his claim that he would sanction my ex-wife if she did not comply with his Court Order. I was inundated with court documents. I had to file additional papers with the court.

On May 21, 2010, we finally came together in court to address my complaint regarding the ex-wife's interference with my parenting time. As you are aware, I filed this complaint two months earlier in March 2010. Now, I was back in court for the third time to address this issue. I represented myself (Pro-se) in this case. This time around, the ex-wife appeared with her attorney.

For openers, the judge questioned the defendant as to why he should consider her request to reconsider his decisions regarding the Court Order dated March 30, 2010. The judge was concerned because she did not respond to the original complaint, which led to that decision. And, she did not appear in court on March 30, 2010. Her attorney responded by lying in that he said she did not respond to my complaint because for the past two weeks the defendant had been hospitalized.

I had a problem with the story line her attorney presented because the judge's Court Order was issued on March 30, 2010. However, May 21, 2010 was the first day we both appeared in court. If she was hospitalized in the past two weeks that would take us back to May 7, 2010. If you look at a calendar, you will see that this date is well after the original court date of March 30, 2010. Somehow the judge let that significant point get past him. The judge did not challenge her attorney on that issue. And, her attorney did not provide any evidence to show that his client had been hospitalized at any time in the recent past. Fortunately for her, the judge did not request that her attorney provide any medical documentation to support that claim.

Next, her attorney asserted that the reason why the defendant has not let me spend any time with my daughter in the past several months is because my daughter is afraid to be with me. He further stated that I say mean things to my daughter and she does not want to be with me. The attorney went on to say that his client is only protecting her child from the father. He has been too aggressive with their daughter.

Then, the judge asked her attorney to show him some "Red flags." The judge was looking for some evidence to support her claim that my daughter does not want to spend overnights with me. Her attorney did not show the judge any red flags. He did not provide any evidence at all. The judge practically begged her attorney to show him a letter of complaint against me from my daughter, a teacher, a nurse, a social worker, or a DYFS investigator. The attorney did not have any evidence to present to the judge. Instead, her attorney kept saying, "He says things to the little girl."

When it was my turn to present, I told the judge that this is a very simple case. Contrary to what the defendant is alleging, there were no problems with my overnight parenting time before I filed the complaint of abuse with DYFS. This is a clear case of retaliation by the defendant. This is her response to me filing the complaint of child abuse with DYFS. There are no other reasons that I should not be able to spend time with my daughter. I further explained to the judge that her attorney did not provide any evidence to support her false allegations. The judge asked the defendant if there were any problems with me prior to my DYFS complaint. She said, "Relatively not."

At that point, I directed the court's attention to the evidence presented in the five Exhibits that I prepared for this case. Please take a look at the information identified as Exhibits A, B, C, D and E, which are outlined on pages 53-68. This is the documentation I utilized to support my position that my daughter is not afraid of me, and she wants to be with me.

<u>Exhibit A</u>: Defendant claimed she did not receive notification of the March 30, 2010 court date. This exhibit shows that a certified package was delivered to her home address by the postal service on three dates (2/24/10, 3/3/10 and 3/9/10). However, she failed to pick up her certified mail at the post office.

Exhibit B: This exhibit shows the cover page of an audible Father's Day card given to me by my daughter. The voice recording says: "Daddy, I love you for all of the wonderful things you've done for me."

Exhibit C: This exhibit shows a picture of my daughter expressing her love for me during one of my parenting time weekends.

<u>Exhibit D</u>: This exhibit shows a Thank You card from my daughter for the laptop computer I gave her as a gift for always doing so well in school.

Dear Daddy,
Thank you for buying me that nice laptop. It's really cool. I am so happy that you were able to afford something so expensive like that computer.

Thank you,

Love,
Taylor

<u>Exhibit E</u>: This exhibit shows a Father's Day card from my daughter that consisted of several pages, which displays her expressions of love and appreciation for me as her father.

6/21/09

Dear Daddy,
I love you so much. If you weren't here I don't know what I would do without the world's best dad like you.

Love,
Taylor Gardner

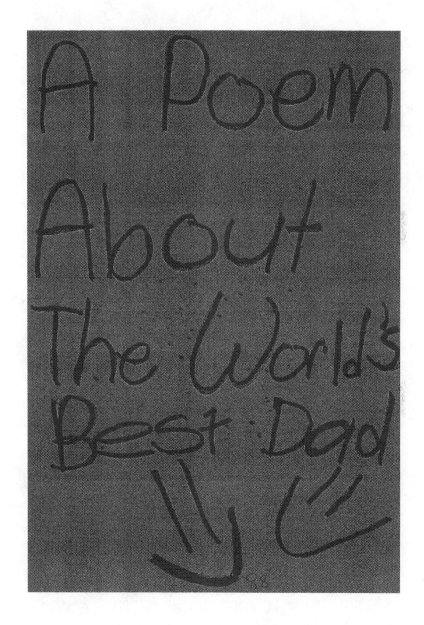

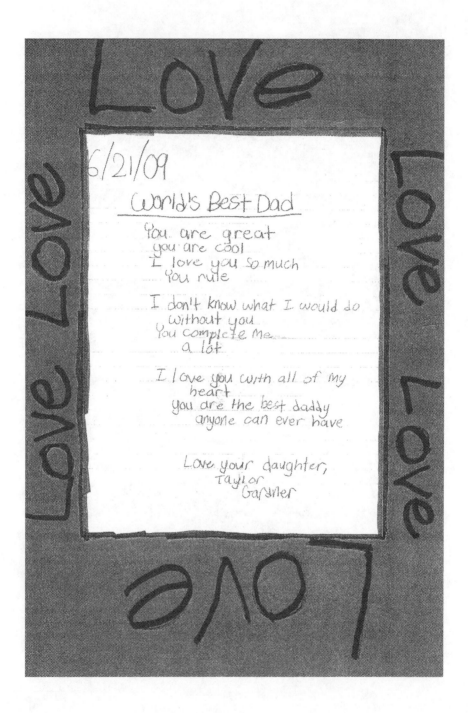

As you can see from your observation of those exhibits, my daughter clearly expresses her love for me. As a matter of fact, in one of her cards she says, "I do not know what I would do without you." I read each and every word that was written in those cards out loud. It was a very compelling moment in the courtroom. I had the attention of everyone present at that time.

After I completed my presentation, the judge called on my ex-wife to respond. Suddenly, she burst into tears. She stood up and put on her best "Academy Award" performance. She cried, as she lied to the judge when she said, "He curses at our daughter. And, that makes her afraid to be with him." When she said that, I was thinking, Hmmm, she is under oath. She is testifying that I am abusive with our daughter. Well, she did not have any evidence. It seemed appropriate that crying would be the next best thing for her to do. After all, it was obvious she had no case against me. At that point, I hoped that her attorney would have advised her to fess up. I wished that he would have advised her to work this out for the benefit of our child. Instead, he took her money knowing that she did not have a leg to stand on. Or, perhaps he knew something that I did not know.

When she finished her testimony (*uh hmm*) performance, her attorney stood up. He continued to do a poor job of advocating for her. He repeatedly said to the judge, "Your honor, he says things to the little girl. He says things to her and she does not want to be with him." Her attorney repeated those false statements too many times for me. I could not tolerate his foolishness anymore.

I stood up in the court room. I spoke directly to her attorney. I told him in a loud voice, "Stop it. Please stop saying that. You have no evidence to support anything you say. You have not said anything specific about what I say to my daughter that would preclude her from wanting to spend time with me." As I continued, I told the attorney, "You are standing here as if you have over heard me say mean things to my daughter." I said, "If you would have heard me say anything to her, you would have heard me tell her how much I love her. You would have heard me tell her how special she is to me." I told the attorney that, "I am a good father, and I will not allow you to drag my fatherhood through the mud. I taught that little girl how to love herself, I taught her how to ride a bike, I taught her how to play basketball, and video games. And, my new wife taught her how to Hula hoop!" Then I said to him, "Need I remind you that you are in a court of law and your client is under oath!" Then, I stopped speaking and started crying. That court room was filled with drama.

The judge said he had heard enough. He also said within the next two weeks he will schedule an "In camera interview" with our daughter. The judge stated that he wanted to find out about our daughter's relationship with her parents. While the judge was speaking, I was overwhelmed by my emotions. I was crying and sobbing like I was at my own funeral. Then the judge asked me if I would accept a reduced parenting time schedule. He offered me one day on alternating Saturday's until he met with my daughter. In my mind that was unacceptable. I asked the judge why should I accept a reduction in my parenting time. I told him that I am currently unemployed. Yet, I am still required to pay 100% of child support. If I fail to do so, I would be incarcerated. The judge and the ex-wife's attorney seemed to be amused by my analogy. The expressions on their faces showed that they did not believe I compared my parenting time to my child support obligation. And for me, this is one of the things that I do not understand about family court. Why are fathers incarcerated when they do not pay child support and mothers do not suffer any consequences when they interfere with fathers parenting time?

The judge asked me again if I would accept his offer to see my daughter every other Saturday, until he completed his investigation. I was adamantly opposed to that option. I did not and I could not respond to the judge. I was totally numb at that moment. Then, the judge told me that he is going to temporarily suspend all of my parenting time.

Although I could not answer the judge due to my emotional state of mind, instead of him leaving things as they were, he suspended my parenting time until he met with my daughter. I was shocked into further submission. I sat in my seat dumb founded by his decision. A few minutes later, I said to the judge that I am very concerned that the defendant now has two more weeks to coerce my daughter into supporting her false allegations. The judge asserted that he would be able to determine whether or not my daughter is telling the truth. He said it would not be hard for him to ascertain whether or not my daughter was under pressure from her mother when he questioned her. However, in my mind, I felt like now I was stuck with my daughter being further subjected to the whims of her mother. In addition, my parenting rights were suspended?

The next two weeks passed in what seemed like forever. This was because the judge did not actually meet with my daughter until three weeks later. When we finally returned to court on June 22, 2010, I was anxious, nervous and quietly excited to see if I would finally receive justice. Based on the facts in this case, and the evidence I presented, it seemed like justice would prevail for me.

The judge entered the court room. He opened by saying that he did meet with my daughter on June 15, 2010 for about 20 minutes. He said that it was a good meeting, and he asked my daughter many questions about her parents. The judge told me that my daughter definitely wants to be with me. He said that she expressed her feelings about me. He also stated that there is no doubt in his mind that she wants to be with me. The judge further stated that he asked my daughter about her relationship with my wife and her family. The judge said my daughter told him she enjoyed her time with my wife and her family. After all of that positive feedback, the judge went on to say that he will not reinstate my overnight parenting time. The judge said, "I would prefer that your daughter ease back into her overnight visits with you." He also said, "My decision is based on what is in the best interest of the child." Consequently, the judge ordered in his final decision that my parenting time would be scheduled for every other Saturday from 12:00pm-8:00pm.

I listened to the judge in total disbelief. In my mind, his decision was a travesty of justice. I cried as I listened to the judge dictate the terms of his Court Order regarding this matter. Then the Law Clerk gave me a copy of the judge's order. I walked out of the court room. To my left, I saw the guilty ex-wife standing with her attorney. She was totally elated that she prevailed once again under false pretenses. The only thing I could think about was what just happened in that courtroom. How is my request to have my overnight visits reinstated not in the best interest of my daughter? There was no evidence presented to support the judge's theory that my daughter needed time to warm up to me. Moreover, the only reason my child had not spent overnights with me was because of the retaliatory actions of her mother when she interfered with my parenting time. In my mind, this is an example of injustice in the highest order. The judge made this decision in June 2010. At that point, I had not spent any overnight parenting time with my daughter since January 2010. Why would my daughter who has spent overnight weekends with me over the past seven years need to ease back into her overnight visits with me?

As you might imagine, I was devastated. With this judge's decision, not only did he take away my overnight weekend parenting time, but also he took away all of my additional overnight visitation that was awarded to me in my original divorce Settlement Agreement. Based on that Settlement Agreement, I was entitled to two weeks of parenting time during the summer months. I was also entitled to have my daughter every other New Years Eve. And, I was entitled to have my daughter every other Thanksgiving holiday, as well.

As a consolation, the judge included in his Court Order that I could reapply for overnight parenting time at a later date. But, I had to request that the judge include that provision in his Court Order. Otherwise, overnight visits with my daughter would be a thing of the past.

On the next page, please see a copy of the judges Court Order dated June 22, 2010.

PREPARED BY THE COURT

FILED
JUN 22 2010

SUPERIOR COURT OF NEW JERSEY
CHANCERY DIVISION
BERGEN COUNTY FAMILY PART
DOCKET NO.: FM-02-686-04

ROBERT T. GARDNER   :

    Plaintiff,   :

vs.   :

    :

Defendant.   :

CIVIL ACTION

ORDER

THIS MATTER having been brought before the Court on June 22, 2010, and in the presence of Robert T. Gardner, Pro Se, and .   Esq. on behalf of defendant, and the Court having had an opportunity to consider the papers, and the parties having had an opportunity to be heard, and for good cause shown;

IT IS ON THIS 22nd day of June, 2010;

ORDERED as follows:

1. Plaintiff shall have parenting time with the minor, Taylor on alternate Saturdays between 12:00 noon and 8:00 pm. This shall begin on June 26, 2010.
2. If the minor has any preplanned activities, the parties are hereby ordered to make arrangements so as to make sure the parenting time is made up or exchanged for a different date. This schedule shall not in any way shape or form limit the plaintiff's parenting time in the case of any specific holiday and/or specific family event.
3. Plaintiff shall be permitted through formal motion to apply for overnight parenting time at a later date.
4. Any and all issues not set forth in this Order are hereby denied without prejudice.

_____ J.S.C.

100

It was a very sad time for me throughout the entire six month ordeal with my ex-wife regarding my fight with her for parenting time. This terrible situation reached its culmination point when I heard the judge's decision on June 22, 2010. I learned that I need more than evidence in family court. Such an unfair decision by a judge in a court of law could only be driven by politics, race and gender bias.

In my better judgment as a human resources professional, I would opine that the judge's actions were tantamount to what happens in corporate America regarding cases of discrimination. When there is no sound business reason to deny a promotion to a qualified person of color, racism usually prevails. In my case, there was no evidence presented by the ex-wife, and there was no justice rendered on my behalf by the judge. Therefore, I could easily conclude that this case was decided based on something other than family law.

As I prepare to close my story on this chapter, I would be remiss in my duties if I did not provide you with an update regarding my parenting time with my daughter. As all good stories go, they usually have a happy ending. I am happy to say this story too will have a happy ending, as well. In accordance with the judge's order, I started my parenting time every other Saturday from 12:00pm-8:00pm. I followed that schedule until the middle of August 2010. Then one day during that month, I received a phone call from my daughter's mother. She called to inform me that my daughter wanted to resume her overnight visits with me. She made a point to say that it would only be for one night every other weekend.

Several weeks later, my daughter requested that she would like to stay overnight with me for two nights on Friday and Saturday. Then, my daughter informed her mother that she wanted to spend part of her Christmas 2010 week off from school at my house too. In April 2011, my daughter informed her mother that she wanted to stay at my house during her Spring Break, which she has done. Once again, things are going well during her overnight visits with me. My daughter is enjoying her time at my house with her baby brother and my new wife. And, just like old times before her mother filed her false claims in family court, my daughter still does not want to go home when our weekends together are over.

Since our relationship has returned to normalcy, during one of our weekends together, I decided to ask my daughter if it was her decision not to spend time with me. Or, did her mother put her up to tell me that she did not want to spend time with me. My daughter told me that during those times her mother would call her into her bedroom. Then her mother would make her sit on her bed and call me. My daughter said, "My mother instructed me to tell you that I did not want to spend any time at your house." My daughter also said, "It made me feel real bad and confused to do that to you daddy." She said, "I wanted to go with you, but my mother made me call and tell you that I did not want to spend any time with you on the weekends." My daughter apologized to me. That brought tears to my eyes. I told my daughter that I totally understand what she experienced with her mother during that time, and she does not owe me an apology. I also tried to make sure that my daughter understood that she should not concern herself with that issue. I did not want my daughter to blame herself for the diabolical and dastardly work that her mother did to hurt me. I wanted my daughter to clear her conscious regarding that experience. If not, that would be a great example of how a child's emotional health could be adversely affected when a parent uses the child as a pawn. My daughter felt terrible about that situation, and she was feeling lots of guilt regarding that incident.

This discussion with my daughter was not only the final piece of evidence that proved my access to her was denied, but also it clearly demonstrates how a child can be the victim of their parent's anger and suffer emotionally in the process.

However, my daughter and I work through those issues. We are not mad at her mother. We are very happy that we are back together again! Our bond will continue to be solidified for all time sake . . .

Expressions of the effects of
Access Denied on the children . . .

The children remember when their fathers were there for them . . .

Lack of Support in Family Court

When my divorce was finally approved and signed by the judge, I thought my ex-wife and I would both move on with our respective lives. It turns out that I was wrong. For eight years, 2003-2010, after our divorce we had been mired in numerous legal battles in the family court system.

When I look back over that period of time, I see that family court has been an extensive uphill journey for me.

During my experience in family court, I often wondered why my abusive ex-wife received all of the favorable decisions from the judges. Her harassing and menacing behavior had been well documented in the annals of family court.

Yet no matter what I reported to the authorities in family court regarding her unlawful behavior, she has never been held accountable.

One would think that if a woman makes false reports to the police, false reports to child welfare agencies, tells lies under oath in court, harasses her ex-husband, and interferes with his parenting time, she should be held accountable for her unlawful behavior.

But, to the contrary, she has not experienced any consequences whatsoever. Since there has not been any repercussions for her, she continues to act as if she has an unfettered right to violate our divorce settlement agreement.

I use to think a lot about why I have not had any success in family court regarding my attempts to address the unlawful behavior of my ex-wife. During that time,

I have spoken to other people regarding their issues with ex-mates and the inequities they have experienced in family court.

I found that I am not alone regarding my troubles with my ex-wife and the unfair treatment that I experienced in family court. The disparity of justice for men in family court seems to permeate throughout the family court system. Although I have spoken to many people about these issues, there is one story that comes to mind that I would like to share with you. After you read this story, I believe you will fully understand the difficulties that come into play with ex-mates, and the agony of having your access denied to your children.

Below is the interview that I conducted with a father who gave me permission to tell you his story. This interview will provide you with a detailed and vivid account of his devastating experiences regarding his fight with his ex-mate to spend time with his daughter. Please note, the individual I interviewed requested that his identity remain anonymous.

The interview:

Q. Where does this story take place?

A. In central New Jersey.

Q. What is your ethnic background?

A. I am African American.

Q. When did this story begin?

A. In 1989, when my oldest daughter was born.

Q. Were you married to the mother of this child?

A. No.

Q. What happened?

A. In 1989, I was involved in a relationship with a Hispanic lady. On or before my eighteenth birthday, I found out she was pregnant. She came from a strict Puerto Rican family. They tried to keep her away from me when it was confirmed that she was pregnant. First, they moved to Florida. Then they moved back to New Jersey shortly before my daughter was born. At the time my daughter was born, I did not know anything about her birth until three days after she was born.

As soon as I found out my daughter was born, I claimed responsibility for her. I made several attempts to talk to my girlfriend's father, but he rejected me. I was not allowed to see my daughter. Her family denied me access to my daughter. I only saw her three or four times in the first year of her life.

During that time, I did not have many chances to talk with the mother of my child. Her family would not let me have much contact with her. Eventually, my relationship with my daughter and her mother came to an end.

After my struggles with my daughter's family in the first year, they took me to court for child support. This was a good thing for me. I had a good job, and it established my parenting rights.

After my parenting rights were established in family court, my ex-girlfriend's family still did not allow me to pick up my daughter on my scheduled parenting time weekends. That resulted in arguments and physical altercations with my ex-girlfriend's father. On the occasions when there were no fights, my daughter would cry when she saw me.

It seemed like my daughter saw me as the bad guy. She remembered the violence associated with my attempts to pick her up on the weekends.

Although family court granted me visitation rights, my ex-girlfriend's parents played lots of games with my parenting time. When my pickup times were scheduled for 2:00 p.m. on Saturdays, my ex-girlfriend's family waited for me to arrive at their house. Then they would drive off with my daughter in their car. They would leave the house so I could not spend any time with my daughter.

Next thing I know, my daughter's mother started dating another man. He got involved, and he assisted my daughter's family with not letting me see my daughter. He also drove away from their house with my daughter in his car when I was scheduled to pick her up. I came to realize that it was their plan to prove in family court that I did not pickup my daughter on time.

I started showing up early for my weekend visits. I wanted to catch them before they left their house. When I arrived early, I could not see my daughter without getting into a physical altercation with either my ex-girlfriend's father or her new boyfriend.

Q. At this point, what thoughts are going through your mind? Did you take your ex-girlfriend to family court to enforce your parenting rights?

A. I was stressed, depressed and very angry. I went to family court many times.

In the beginning, it seemed like the court process was fair. However, I did not receive any support from family court. The judge always threatened to sanction my daughter's mother for not allowing me to see my daughter. But no action was ever taken by any of the judges to stop her from interfering with my parenting time.

Q. What else happened?

A. My daughter's family refused to communicate with me. They showed a total disregard for me and my desire to spend time with my daughter. As time went on, I continued to have arguments with the new boyfriend and my ex-girlfriend's father. All I wanted to do was spend time with my daughter. They would not allow me to be with my daughter at all.

Then I heard that my daughter's mother was being physically abused by her boyfriend. He put fear in my daughter's mother, which made it even more difficult for me to see my daughter.

On one occasion, I tried to talk to my daughter's mother at her house. I wanted to find out why she would not let me see my daughter. Her father interrupted our discussion. I got into another argument with him. On that same day, her boyfriend also got involved. Then I had another physical altercation with the boyfriend. This fight was about the fact that they leave the house every time I come to pick up my daughter.

Rarely did they make my daughter available to me for my scheduled pick up times. And the times when they did allow me to see her, my daughter always cried when she saw me.

I attributed my daughter's crying to the fact that all of my visits were associated with violence. I had either arguments or actual fists fights with members of her mother's family. I think my daughter saw me as a troublemaker.

Q. When you went to court to address these issues, did you have an attorney?

A. No, I represented myself.

Q. Did you ever fall behind in your child support payments?

A. Yes.

Q. What happened?

A. I was arrested. I was incarcerated at least three times even though my parenting rights were never honored by the judges in family court.

Q. How did you feel about being incarcerated? And how did you feel about everything you experienced and you did not receive any support from family court?

A. I felt like my head was going to burst. I was filled with so much anger and stress over this situation.

Q. What else happened?

A. My daughter's mother married her abusive boyfriend. And he got more involved with trying to keep me away from my daughter. After they got married, it seemed like he believed he had more rights to fight against me. Every time I went to pick up my daughter, I had a fight with her mother and her mother's husband. As a result, my daughter never warmed up to me.

The next time I went to court to enforce my visitation rights, the judge stressed to my daughter's mother that he would incarcerate her if she did not comply with his court order. After we left family court, my daughter's mother was very upset by the threats of incarceration that she received from the judge. She cried as she left the court room.

And because she was crying, her husband got upset with me. He jumped in my face. He said I was the blame for what the judge said to his wife. I got into another fight with him right outside of the courtroom. Both he and I were arrested. Eventually, I was released because some of the people who witnessed this incident spoke up for me. I dropped the charges of assault against him.

After the fight with my daughter's stepfather, I still tried to see my daughter on my parenting time weekends. But, both her mother and stepfather continued to deny me access to my daughter. Even though the judge frequently threatened to incarcerate my daughter's mother, she continued to violate the judges' court orders. And, as it turned out, the judge did not incarcerate her for refusing to comply with any of his court orders.

Q. Approximately how old was your daughter when these events occurred?

A. She was eight years old.

Q. At this point, your daughter is eight years old. You have never had an easy time trying to spend time with her. What made you continue to fight for so long, and so hard to see your daughter?

A. Yes, I did continue my fight to see my daughter. I bought her clothes that her mother and stepfather could not afford. And my daughter has these big pretty eyes. It broke my heart to see her cry every time she saw me. My other children love me to death. So I worked hard to get the love of my first child. I never had a chance to give her any real love without a fight.

And, more and more, I started feeling like my head was going to explode. I was so angry and hurt by this situation.

Q. What happened next?

A. As time went on, my daughter started to relax a bit when I came to see her. She started to connect my visits with trips to toy stores, the ice cream parlors, and play dates with my other children.

But the fights with her stepfather continued. However, my daughter's mother started to communicate with me behind her husband's back. She would call me and tell me how my daughter was doing in school.

Q. What, if anything, did family court do about this situation?

A. I stopped going to court because it was a waste of my time. For eight years, I had been in and out of family court. I received absolutely no support. I had court orders that stated I could spend time with my daughter every other weekend. But, because of all of the fighting with my ex-girlfriend and her husband, I only saw my daughter every now and then.

Sometimes me and my daughter would talk on the telephone. And whenever I did get an opportunity to speak to my daughter, I would explain to her that her stepfather does not like me. I would tell her that I am not a bad person. I would also tell her that I wanted to be her father. I would tell her that she would understand things better when she grows up. I wanted my daughter to know that I tried everything to be in her life. And all I ever wanted to do was be a good father to my daughter.

However, nothing I said to my daughter seemed to work. I still paid my child support, which was about $200 a week. I paid more than I was legally required to pay. I thought it would draw my daughter closer to me if I bought her things that she wanted. Then there were times when it was alright with her mother and stepfather for my daughter to call me when she wanted things that they could not afford.

When my daughter was ten years old, she called to inform me that she wanted to drop my last name. She wanted to change her last name to the same last name as her stepfather, her mother and her little brother.

Instead of my daughter getting closer to me, she requested that I give her permission to drop my last name. I was totally shocked by this situation.

Then I asked to speak to her mother about the name change. Her mother confirmed my daughter's feelings about the name change issue in their house. I asked my daughter's mother to put my daughter back on the phone. I told my daughter that if she really wanted to drop my name, I would allow her to drop my last name.

Q. Ten years have passed regarding your fight to spend time with your daughter. What were your feelings at that point in time?

A. It hurt me a lot when my daughter told me she decided to drop my last name. I tried hard to suppress my feelings about this situation. However, I understood that they were also trying to get me out of my daughter's life.

Q. At this point, were you somewhat conditioned to not having your daughter in your life, and if so, was it easier for you to deal with these new issues?

A. It was never easy for me to deal with any of these issues. However, I was starting to get to the point where I stopped fighting so much for my visitation rights. I was tired and I was depressed.

Whenever I had my other kids, I still called my daughter's mother to see if I could spend time with my daughter. I gave my daughter's mother the telephone numbers of my other children. I wanted my daughter to stay in touch with her other brothers and sisters.

After the issues seemed to have slowed down, the fights started again. Then, I received a notice to appear in family court. This notice was submitted by my daughter's mother to request that my daughter's last name be changed to the same last name as her stepfather.

In addition, I was angered by the fact that there was also a request for me to give up my parenting rights. I was really pissed off. This issue was not discussed at all during any of our previous talks regarding the name change.

After I read the letter several times, I called my daughter's mother to discuss this matter. We argued for a long time on the telephone. Before our court date regarding this issue, we had about 10 more fights over the parenting rights issue. At this point, whenever I was scheduled to see my daughter prior to the court date, I would get into physical altercations with her stepfather. Subsequently, they did not let me see my daughter until we were all in court together.

Q. After all you had been through in this situation, did you think for one moment that it might be a good idea for you to give up your parenting rights?

A. No. I did not think for one minute that it was a good idea to give up my parenting rights. As I said earlier, we had about ten fights before the court date. On the day we went to court, we argued in the hallway, and we argued in front of the mediator. I said no to everybody who asked me to give up my parenting rights. I told them that I pay child support. I want to be in my daughter's life. I love my daughter.

As we were arguing, my daughter took their side. As the discussions continued, it was brought up by the mediator that I would not have to pay child support if I gave up my rights.

At the same time, I started thinking about what my doctor told me on a recent visit to his office. My doctor advised me that the best remedy for me in this situation was to just say, "F—k it."

My doctor said, "You cannot control something that is out of your hands. You have to just say f—k it."

On the day we were in court, I was already taking the stress medicine that was prescribed by my doctor due to this situation. My daughter was nine years old when I started taking stress medication. The funny thing about this medicine is when I was a child, I used to get bad headaches. After I started taking medicine for those headaches, they went away.

Due to this situation, the headaches came back. However, this new medication made me drowsy and tired. I spoke to my doctor about the side effects of this medication. I told my doctor I could not continue to take these meds because of the side effects. I asked him if he could prescribe a different medication. My doctor told me that if I walked away from this situation, he would not have to prescribe any medication for me.

Q. Your doctor actually said that your best remedy is to say, "F—k it," and let this situation go?

A. Yes. He said, "If you can't fix it, stop stressing about things that are out of your control."

So these things were on my mind while we were in court. I started thinking about the idea of not paying child support. I looked back on all the trouble I had in connection with my battle to spend time with my daughter. I thought about all the stress this situation has caused me. It seemed like it made good sense for me to give up my parenting rights. I decided to sign the papers to give up my rights to my daughter.

Q. Did you have a chance to say good-bye to your daughter?

A. No. Her mother and stepfather did not allow me to see her when the hearing ended. Some time went by before we received the judge's final order. I was not allowed to see my daughter during that time. So I did not have a chance to say anything to my daughter. And, it hurt me very much.

However, I realized it was better for me to let go. I had a chance to reduce the stress in my life. As a matter of fact, I did not speak to my daughter for two years after I gave up my parenting rights. But, I continued to call my daughter's mother. I tried to see if I could spend time with my daughter. Her stepfather and mother would not let me see her.

Then one day I received a call from one of my relatives. My aunt told me that she saw my daughter around the corner from her house. She said my daughter was visiting her stepfather's mother.

After I hung up the telephone, I jumped into my car and drove to Keyport, New Jersey. I went to see my daughter. I was very happy that I had another chance to finally see my daughter again. However, when I arrived, I noticed right away that she was not happy to see me. And, she was very reluctant to interact with me. My daughter acted as if she was told not to respond to me in a loving way. I saw it in her face. She was not excited to see me, and so after a few minutes, I left with a broken heart.

Q. Did you have any other opportunities to see your daughter after that time?

A. A significant period of time passed before I saw my daughter again. The next time I saw her, she was a teenager. I tried to interact with her, but I did not have any success. I could not break through the barriers she put up to keep me away.

After that I began to call my aunt on a regular basis, since she lived around the corner from my daughter's step-grandmother's house. I wanted to find out if my daughter might be in the area for a visit. Eventually, I was able to get a contact number to my daughter's mother's house. I called and spoke to my daughter.

When her stepfather found out I called, he changed the telephone number. In fact, that became the cycle. Whenever I would find out the new telephone number, the stepfather would change the telephone number.

This continued to the point where my daughter became accustomed to not talking to me. It seemed like I was totally eliminated from her life.

Q. How old was your daughter at this point in time?

A. She was 14 years old.

Q. How old is your daughter today (5/4/10)?

A. She is twenty-one years old.

Q. Have you seen your daughter at all since the last time you saw her in Keyport, New Jersey?

A. Yes, I have seen her.

Q. Has she tried to get closer to you now that she has grown up?

A. No. She only reaches out to me every now and then. Actually, it is more of a case of me reaching out to her. She does not reach out to me.

Now she lives independent from her mother. To this date, we do not have an active relationship. We are at the point where I will get her phone number from one of my other children, and I call her. Then she changes her telephone number.

The only thing I can really be happy about is that she stays in touch with my other children. The fact that she stays in touch with her brothers and sisters is very important to me. Unfortunately, at the age of 21, she still will not connect with me.

Q. Have you been able to move on now that your daughter has grown up, and she has no interest in getting to know you?

A. I regret that this situation has turned out the way it did. It use to beat the heck out of me. I have thought a lot about what kind of man am I that I would give up my parenting rights. What kind of man would do that? I hear people say all the time that they would never give up their parenting rights. I felt like scum.

After I signed away my parenting rights, I let that beat me up for years.

Q. What happened to you?

A. I would get depressed at times when I thought about what I did. It hurt so much. I felt terrible about giving up my parenting rights. To make matters worse, there were times I would reach out to my daughter and speak to her on the telephone.

The next time I called her, I would find out that she changed her telephone number. My daughter changed her telephone numbers just like her stepfather use to do when I called his house.

Q. Are you mad at your daughter's mother for the way she has denied your access to your child?

A. No. I realize that she was controlled by both of her parents and her husband. Funny thing now, her parents speak to me when I see them around town. My daughter's mother's brothers and sisters always spoke to me. They knew that I was a responsible person. They also knew I wanted to be a father to my daughter.

Q. What have you learned from this experience?

A. There is no justice in family court. They did nothing to ensure that I ever spent any time with my daughter. And as I said before, I was incarcerated three times when I fell behind in my child support payments. This usually happened when I was unemployed because I was laid off from different jobs over the years.

Q. Do you feel you were discriminated against as a man in family court?

A. I felt discriminated against as a black man and as a man. It seems to me that if a person does not have money and a high-powered attorney, they do not stand a chance in family court. I felt that way back then. I still feel that way now. I am still tied up in family court with the mother of one of my other children.

The courts require me to provide all kinds of financial information. However, the mother of my other child does not provide any documentation. The courts make decisions against me based on what she says and not what documentation she provides.

Q. Do you have any final thoughts regarding this tragic situation, whereby you have fought for more than 20 years to spend time with your daughter, and you have been turned away over and over again?

A. Yes, the first thing is that I am pleased that my work to have my children know one another has paid off. My oldest daughter and my youngest daughter have a relationship.

I do not know where my oldest daughter lives today. I hear that she is getting married. I always wanted to have a relationship with my daughter. I still regret giving up my parenting rights.

My youngest son was very disturbed by the fact that I gave up my rights. I explained to him what I went through and what led to my decision to give up my rights.

I have only seen my 21 year-old daughter two times in the past three years. When we see each other, we hug and say we love each other. I am not sure that her message of love is sincere. We talk about getting together. When I call her, she always makes excuses about why she cannot get together with me. In addition, she never gets back to me about a new time for us to get together.

I realize that she is grown now. I cannot force her to spend time with me. I have to let her go her own way. I will always be there for her if she needs me. I still love my daughter with all of my heart!

Conclusion of Interview

As I wrap up this interview, I would like to say that I cannot thank you enough for digging real deep to take my readers through that painful journey. Your fight for your daughter is an amazing story and you put forth a tremendous effort to be her father. I can see that you still feel some pain from that experience.

It is an enormous tragedy that you missed out on the opportunity to be a father to your daughter. And it is a crime that your daughter's family worked so hard to keep you from your child—all based on their racist, selfish, and ignorant behavior.

Apparently, they had no idea regarding the emotional damage they may have caused for your daughter that could affect her for the rest of her life. And, your ex-girlfriend's family did not seem to understand the importance of a father in a child's life. While they fought to keep you away, they simultaneously denied your daughter a chance to learn about her father's heritage. That is a very important aspect of her emotional health, as it pertains to her self awareness.

At this time, I would like to wish you the best of everything, as you go forward in your future dealings with your other children. Thank you very much for sharing your story. I hope and pray that one day your daughter will come home to see about her father . . .

After your review of this story, can you imagine what this child must have experienced during that time. This young lady may have been brainwashed in a coercive fashion by her own family members. Perhaps, she may have even been threatened by these people with some sort of corporal punishment if she did not cooperate with their demands to disassociate herself from her biological father.

Here you have an innocent child who was for the most part abducted from her father. He spent 20 plus years trying to demonstrate to his daughter that he wanted to be in her life. However, as a little girl, she was manipulated, controlled and denied a life with her biological father due to the diabolical actions of her mother, her grandfather and her abusive step father. To what extent does a child benefit when denied access to their biological father while at the same time, the child is being controlled by their abusive stepfather? Abusive parents are not known to be very nurturing or loving.

This is a very sad story that demonstrates the far reaching devastating effects on the life and emotional health of children. Today, this little girl who is now a grown woman has to go through her life's journey carrying the onerous burden of denying that her father exists. This young lady never had the opportunity to decide for herself whether or not she would want her biological father to be a part of her life. This void in her life may never be filled. And that emptiness sometimes leads to feelings of life long guilt, shame and denial that can stifle her from becoming a productive member of society.

Child Pawn

Definitively speaking, "Child Pawn" is what I consider to be one of the most severe consequences for children when the relationship between their parents end on bad terms. A typical case of child pawn occurs when the primary (custodial) parent is angered by the termination of a relationship with an ex-mate who is the other parent of the children born from that relationship. In these cases, the angry parent does not allow the other parent to spend time with their children after their relationship has ended.

Quite often, child pawn evolves into a series of insidious and diabolical acts, which are initiated by the angry parent. These acts are carried out over an extended period of time by the angry parent. That parent uses the children as a weapon to hurt the other parent for breaking off their relationship. And, the diabolical acts vary in degrees of anger, evil and insane behavior displayed by the angry parent. These acts include but are not limited to denying access to the children, brain washing the children to dislike the other parent, discrediting the other parent, and abusing the children both physically and emotionally to coerce them to support the behavior of the angry parent.

In other cases regarding child pawn, the children may be told over and over again that their other parent does not want to spend any time with them. When in fact, the other parent does want to be with their children. However, that parent is unable to spend time with their children because their access has been denied by the angry parent. This type of angry parenting can result in an enormous amount of emotional trauma for the children subjected to the ways and means of their angry parent. In addition, when children are caught in the crossfire between the wrath of one angry parent and denied access to their other parent, their emotional health can be damaged in many ways.

In addition to low self esteem, the lack of self love and the overall feelings of guilt that may arise for children when used as pawns, sometimes the children blame themselves when they cannot spend any time with their other parent. These feelings may lead to anger and depression on the part of the children. This can have a negative affect on the behavior of these children in school and also have an adverse impact on their academic performance, as well. Children tend to act out when they are angry about unexplained voids in their lives regarding an absent parent. Further, life as a pawn for a child can be very confusing. They may be told by their angry parent to disown their other parent because he does not love them. The children can be easily confused by such false statements, since they have loving memories of the time spent with their fathers. The children want to feel good about both of their parents. These children also witness the angry parent doing all of the bad things to hurt the other parent. And if the children were not exposed to the constant negative energy from the angry parent, the children would have a better chance to be emotionally healthy. Instead, they may find themselves struggling with feelings of guilt, shame, and confusion because they were coerced by their angry parent to conspire with them to hurt and disrupt the life of their other parent. This may present a huge conflict for the children because they want to love their other parent too.

On the next few pages, you will read about the real life experience of a 12 year old child, as told by his mother in my interview with her. She describes the intimate details of how her son has been caught in the quagmire of a devastating game of child pawn being played by her ex-husband. Hopefully, as you read this story, you will come to understand the damaging effects that child pawn can have on the emotional health of a child.

Although this book is intended to reveal the suffrage of fathers regarding child pawn, I felt obligated to share the story of a mother whose child has been victimized, by his father, in acts of child pawn. Over the years, it has been well documented that more often than not fathers are usually subjected to the whims of their baby mamas when it comes to not being able to spend time with their children. However, child pawn is child pawn and it can devastate the lives of our children no matter which parent carries out their plan to use children as pawns to hurt the other parent.

The Interview

Q. What is your name?

A. I would like to remain anonymous.

Q. Where does this story take place?

A. In the New York Tri-State Area.

Q. What is your ethnic background?

A. I am an African American female.

Q. How long were you married?

A. I was married from 1993-2007, which totals 14 years of marriage.

Q. Why did your marriage end in divorce?

A. At first I really did not know why my marriage ended in divorce. I was somewhat baffled by the whole thing.

After I thought about it, I think the number one issue was money. The other reasons for my divorce were a lack of communication, growing apart from one another, and having different values.

Most of all, I think my ex-husband was a passive-aggressive individual. He was not happy, and he pretended that he was.

Q. I understand from previous discussions with you that your ex-husband asked for the divorce. While at the same time, he is not letting you go. You have maintained that he continues to harass and menace you. Please talk about that situation?

A. Yes, he did initiate the divorce process. I have been fully cooperative with his wishes regarding the divorce. However, I have concerns regarding three demands that he has made in his divorce papers. I will not comply with any of those demands. He wants full custody of our son. He demands that I only see my son on the weekends. And, he wants me to pay him child support. These are the issues that are being contested by me in our divorce proceedings.

Other than those issues, I have been willing to fully cooperate with his wishes. However, there have been numerous additional legal motions filed by him. He has had several attorneys handle his case. It has turned into a long-drawn out battle.

Q. How did your son handle the idea of his parents getting a divorce?

A. My son is currently in his second series of therapeutic counseling sessions regarding the issues related to this divorce. Prior to our divorce, my son use to say that he was the happiest child in the world. Now he says that he is just miserable and depressed.

Q. How old was your son when the divorce process began?

A. He was eight years old.

Q. How old is your son now?

A. He is 12 years old. It has been four years of involvement with the divorce process.

Q. Can you talk about some of the things your ex-husband has done to exact revenge on you during your experience with the divorce process?

A. The first thing he did was try to cripple me financially. He wanted me to move out of the house. This would have had a significant impact on my finances. I would have had to find a place to live and start over again. In addition, he would have filed a claim for child support if I would have moved out of the house.

Also, while we resided in the house together during the early stages of our divorce, he constantly tried to provoke me into a domestic violence situation. I stopped talking to him. I felt that if we did not talk, then we could not argue. Then he started making claims in family court that I did not live in the house.

He did that because I would only be home when my son was in the house. Other than that, I would go to the gym, the library, and other places to avoid him. I did not want to be home alone with him.

Q. Has your ex-husband's behavior affected your son mentally, emotionally, educationally, physically, and otherwise? If so, please talk about each topic separately.

A. With regard to the mental aspect, my son now bites his nails. He is fidgety, and he has been diagnosed with ADHD (Attention Deficit Hyperactivity Disorder). My son is currently reading at a third-grade level, and he is in the sixth grade.

In addition, my son now has a reading disorder. He finds it very hard to concentrate. And based on the fact that he also has a very high IQ (intellectual capacity), all of this has been very frustrating for me.

His father has done many things to sabotage his educational activities. He made sure that my son did not go to mandatory summer school. He has not followed through on our son's homework assignments. He does not check to see if the homework assignments are completed.

He has not made a tuition payment to our son's school in quite some time. Just because we are divorcing does not mean he should stop paying for the education of our son.

He is also in deep denial regarding our son having a reading disorder. He has not wanted to address this issue. While I have tried to place our son in summer reading programs, my ex-husband has said I was a mean mother. He told me that our son is going to grow up hating me.

There was a period of time when my son would not hug me. Nor would he show me any signs of affection. My ex-husband claims that because of me our son has great animosity towards women.

Q. Before we go any further, I would like to revisit the fact that you said your son has a third-grade reading level.

A. Yes, he does, and he is in the sixth grade. However, he is dealing with this issue of ADHD. The good thing is that my son does have a high IQ, and if he is placed in a supportive environment, he would rise above that condition.

If my son had a one-on-one tutor, he would be able to get back on track with his grade appropriate reading scores. This is what I have been working toward and trying to provide for my son.

Q. What do you attribute to the issues regarding your son's educational challenges?

A. I attribute the issues we are dealing with to his father. He and I have different values regarding the education of our child.

His father is not supportive at all regarding our son's educational goals. I am the parent who espouses the view that our child should be college educated.

His father tells our son that he does not have to go to college. He told our son that all you have to do is get a job and try to make a lot of money.

Even when our son's teachers inform his father about the inappropriate behavior of our son in school, the father says that the teachers are wrong. He is in complete denial regarding any of the issues related to our son in school.

Behavioral issues with our son began to arise during the early stages of our divorce. I had to deal with some tough issues in school regarding my son. Things started to go bad for my son in the fourth grade. I had to rearrange my entire schedule to be available to sit in school with my son. Based on the behavior that had been reported by the school, I had to observe his behavior while he sat in his classrooms.

When my son was in the fifth grade, he did very well. He had a male teacher and he made the honor roll. However, during the winter recess when custody became an issue, my son was suspended from school twice within a short period of time.

The bottom line is that all of the issues regarding our son in school could change for the better, if he was in a more supportive environment. In addition, my son would also have to be placed in remedial programs to reinforce his academic work in school.

Q. What were the issues regarding his behavior that led to two suspensions from school?

A. My son would totally disrespect the instructions given to him by his teachers. If he was told to sit down, he would not sit down. He blatantly disregarded the authority of his teachers.

Q. Do you believe your son's behavior in school could be attributed to the fact that he has been affected by the actions of his parents?

A. I believe my son is confused. He says that he would like to live with his dad. But he knows that is not the place for him to live because it is a very negative environment. My son's father lives with his father. They do not keep their house clean, and they do not keep food in the house. My son does not eat right when he is with his father. However, he is still very loyal to his dad. I am not sure if his dad is threatening him to say that he would rather live with his father. The times when my son has either been suspended from school or when he has acted out in school was during the time he was with his father. My son may think his behavior is acceptable to his dad.

However, I have explained to my son that inappropriate behavior in school is not acceptable at any time. I told him that it does not matter which parent he is living with.

Q. Has this situation with your ex-husband affected your son emotionally regarding his self-esteem?

A. Yes. When my son returned home from winter break with his father, he was a totally different child. Before my son went to his father's house, he was fun, loving, and feeling good. Upon his return to school, I started getting complaints from his teachers. The reports from the teachers were that my son was not himself. He was withdrawn, lethargic, and sleepy in class.

My son even told me that he was depressed. He would walk around the house like he was in a daze. I started to worry. I had concerns that his behavior might be related to drugs. I just did not know what was going on with him. He slept with me for two weeks when he returned home. He was very clingy with me during that period.

I began to pray with him in church. I spent a lot of individual time with him too. He also had 20 hours of one-on-one tutoring regarding his schoolwork. We visited museums and participated in other activities.

All of these activities restored my son to the person he was before winter break. At first, he did not want to participate in any of the programs I scheduled for him. Now, he does not want to leave the programs when I pick him up. His self-esteem has boosted to a higher level. He is doing much better in school. The change of environment from his father's house to my house has worked out great.

However, although my son has improved in school, I have noticed that his performance in school fluctuates like the stock market. In his first semester back to school, he made the honor roll. The next semester, his grades dropped somewhat. Then they rose again.

I believe his performance in school is related to the fact that we are now revisiting the custody issue between me and his father. Now that this issue has come up again, I think it is affecting my son in a negative way.

These types of issues are hard to prove in family court. The courts are only interested in the physical scars on a child's body. The courts are not interested in the emotional scars that a child may have related to what they experience with a parent. These are the things that really hurt our children, and it is really hard to prove.

Q. Are there any issues with your son from a physical perspective? Does he actively play in the park with other children?

A. From a physical standpoint, when he comes back home to me from his father's house, he is always hungry, and he is always sleepy. Those two things seem to be the main issues.

His father has him playing basketball on four different teams. This is also affecting his schoolwork. Once again, his homework is not getting done. His father's priorities are not in order. Everything is basketball and more basketball. For me, school should come first.

Q. Let's talk about some of your experiences in family court. How has family court helped or hurt your situation?

A. Overall, family court has hurt my situation. I wonder what would have happened to me if I did not have my education, financial resources, and the time. I am not sure where I would be in that process. I have had to put my business and my life on hold. In family court, I am always in defending mode refuting the claims of my ex-husband. I had to develop a "Custody kit" where I maintain all of my court-related documents and evidence from A-Z. This way I am always prepared when I go to court.

If I did not have common sense and the resources, I could have been railroaded in court by the false claims of my ex-husband. I have been in and out of court regarding my divorce for the past four years (2007-2011).

Q. What kind of money have you spent during your involvement with the divorce process?

A. I have spent $80,000.

Q. Did you say $80,000?

A. Yes, I did.

Q. Are you done yet with spending money regarding the expenses you have in connection to family court?

A. I am not spending any more money. Now, the state of New York is going to provide funds for me regarding my family court issues. I now have a court-appointed 18B lawyer. He and I have been working very well together. He has made a significant impact on the reduction of my expenses related to my case in family court.

Over the past four years, I have spent an inordinate amount of money and time on my case. On the flip side of this, I have lost approximately $100,000 in revenue from my business. As I said earlier, I had to put my business endeavors on hold to deal with the challenges presented by my ex-husband.

Q. After all of the time and money spent, have your issues been resolved?

A. No. But I am in a better place in that I was able to have my ex-husband removed from the house. I have been able to get financial support. And, I currently have a custody agreement in place.

Q. Please share your ideas about how you could have helped this situation to be less intense?

A. I asked myself that question thousands of times. Honestly, I cannot give you an answer to that question.

Q. What lessons have you learned from this experience?

A. With regard to the lessons I have learned throughout this journey, I have become a better person as far as being really tough. I did not know that I could be that tough. You know what they say—"If it does not kill you, it will make you stronger."

I realize now that I am really strong. I learned some things about myself that I did not know. I found out that I am very resourceful. I am very creative. And most of all, I was able to get closer to God.

Q. Is there something you can share with my readers to help them avoid the pain and suffering that you and your son have experienced?

A. What I would like to share with people is that they should love their children as much as they can during these times. Look at them in their eyes and talk to them from your heart, as if you are talking to God. This is necessary because the children are the victims. They did not ask for all of this drama. The parents are going through the divorce process, not the children.

Ex-mates should try hard to reconcile their differences outside of court. They should try not to use the court system. I would have been happy to settle our differences out of court. My ex-husband chose to go through the legal system.

Also, take care of yourself during this process. You will need a support system. Develop a strong relationship with God. Do not let yourself go. I did not let my nails go. I did not let my hair go. I always had my body massaged. I exercised and maintained a good diet. I enjoyed comedy shows and movies. Try your best to continue the lifestyle that was in place before things went bad in your marriage. I have learned the best way to get back at my enemy is to look good and do good.

Q. You have already touched on some of the points covered in my next question.

However, I would like to ask you more specifically, what have you done to be emotionally stable and stay strong in the presence of your son?

A. My son and I go to Bible study every Monday night. I have a parenting Bible that we read and have discussions about. We talk openly. Any question he asks me, I do my best to find an answer for him. We do projects together on the computer. We explore the Internet to find "Do it yourself" projects. We work together at things that bring us happiness.

And the things we do together do not involve spending a lot of money. We ride our bikes. We go roller-skating together. We swim together, and we race each other in the pool. These things bring smiles to my son's face. That is a great stress reliever for me.

I really guard my parenting time. I do not hang out with my girlfriends. I do not date my boyfriend when I have my son with me. My focus is on him during our time together.

I do make time for myself when we are together after he is squared away. I do things to keep him filled. I do not try to compete with his father. That could be a recipe for disaster. All my son wants is love and attention. That does not cost anything.

Q. Have you ever been impatient with your son because of the stress related to your family court cases?

A. Yes, I have been impatient with him at times regarding my experience in family court. In the beginning I was stressed when I spent time with him close to scheduled court dates. However, now when I have him, I reduce the things on my schedule. I free myself from being stressed by not having too many things to do during our time together.

I make sure I have a treat for myself after a court date. And, I prefer not to have my son immediately following a court date. I have to do something for myself to "Detoxify me." If I am scheduled to have my son on the same day of a scheduled date in family court, I order Chinese food. Then we go to bed. We play a game to see who can go to sleep first.

Conclusion of Interview

As we close out this interview, I have to say that it seems like you have become an expert in finding ways to take care of both you and your son during a very difficult time. This interview has been quite a learning experience for me and hopefully for my readers, as well. The way you have turned your negative experiences into positive outcomes has been magnificent. I admire the way you have handled yourself during some very tough times.

Q. Is there anything else you would like to share that I have not asked you regarding your experience with the divorce process and its affect on your son?

A. If you know your mate is confrontational or may have problems letting you go, you should consider therapy. You will need to prepare yourself for the breakup. This may be necessary because you have been living with somebody for an extended period of time. Sometimes even change for the better can be painful. Through therapy, you may get some strategies for making the change less painful.

Try to minimize confrontations with your soon-to-be ex-mate as much as possible. Some things you will have to ignore. Do not respond to everything they say. Do not dignify every comment with a response. I found that the best way to deal with this situation is by not saying anything. No answer is an answer.

This process may make you question yourself. You always have to defend yourself. You always have to prove yourself in court. It can be overwhelming. You have to know that you are doing the right thing when you try to end a bad relationship. It is the person who will not let go that causes all or most of the trouble. Stay true to who you are.

I thank God for technology. I taped everything he said. I recorded things he said that led to him being removed from the house. You must document, document, and document everything.

I would like to take this opportunity to thank you very much for the time you took to share your story. Your experience has been quite an adventure. My hope is that people will learn from your experience and think more about their children, and less about the fight to hurt each other. You have made a tremendous contribution to the purpose of this book, which is intended to educate people about the horrors of child pawn.

To sum it all up, here we have a child caught in the grip of anger between both of his parents. Unfortunately for this child, his father has a heavy negative influence over his life. That negative influence has been exercised by the father to use his child as a pawn. In doing so, he has worked against every positive effort the mother has made to provide a supportive environment for their child during a very tough divorce process. Since the supportive environment has not been provided by both parents, now they have a child acting out in school. A child who has been depressed. A child who has been diagnosed with Attention Deficit Hyperactive Disorder. A child who is reading three grade levels below his age group and sometimes he bites his nails when he feels anxious. A child that has been told by his father that he does not need a college education. And most of all, they have a child who is not able to be all that he could be as a 12 year old. Instead, they have a child who has been incarcerated by the shackles of parental warfare. Nobody ever wins these types of battles and the biggest losers are always the children.

DYFS or Die First
The Only Option for Children in New Jersey

In the many cases of child abuse that are reported in the state of New Jersey, DYFS is the exclusive decision maker on whether or not our children have been abused by their parents. Over the years, the record shows that DYFS has made a number of bad decisions regarding the welfare and safety of our children. Unfortunately, some of their bad decisions have resulted in the deaths of abused children.

For some strange reason, DYFS does not consider the severity of abuse from an emotional standpoint. Quite often, in the face of severe emotional and physical abuse, DYFS allows minor children to decide whether or not they want to return home to a parent or parents who have brutalized them physically and emotionally.

The only standard utilized in these decisions is the evidence of scars or bruises on a child's body after a severe beating. As we know, some bruises and scars tend to disappear on a child's body after a short period of time. Therefore, bad decisions are made to place children back into the homes where their abusive parent(s) have free rein to kill them either emotionally or physically.

Earlier in this book, I informed you that there was somewhat of a happy ending to the madness my daughter and I experienced regarding her mother's abusive ways. However, in the spring of 2012, my daughter informed me that she was experiencing what I consider to be some outrageous abusive behavior at the hands of her mother. During that period, on my parenting time weekends, I asked my daughter to list the details of those events so we could compile an in depth body of work regarding the many different ways her mother is abusing her. I wanted to make sure that when I reported these abusive acts to DYFS, there would be no question that my daughter is being abused by her mother.

As you may recall in chapter 2, I told you a story about the complaint of abuse I filed with DYFS against my daughter's mother when she put a bar of soap in my daughter's mouth and spanked her. DYFS investigated this matter and determined that it was not abuse. DYFS informed me that they consider abuse to be determined by the "Black and Blue marks" that appear on a child's body after a physical beating by a parent.

Essentially, DYFS disregards the black and blue marks on a child's memory after they have been emotionally abused by either one of their parents during their childhood. During our life course, it is the trauma that we experience in our childhood from either sexual or emotional abuse that we as individuals carry with us throughout our lives. If these issues are not resolved, they can become a major obstacle for us to find happiness with ourselves and in many of our adult relationships.

In so many cases, our unresolved issues are the impetus for our dysfunctional relationships with our mates. There are so many instances where emotional abuse leads to dysfunctional behavior and bad emotional health for the victims of this type of abuse. When children are frequently tormented by their parents, those abusive experiences may have life long negative effects on their emotional health. And yet, DYFS chalks emotional abuse up to just another way that parents may discipline their children.

On August 17, 2012, I called DYFS again to file a claim of abuse against my daughter's mother. My report was based on the incidents, listed below, that were reported to me by my daughter between the months of April 2012 - August 2012. Later that day, DYFS sent an investigator to my house to meet with my daughter. Fortunately, my daughter had the courage to tell the investigator about the details regarding her life at home with her mother. Subsequently, I met with the same investigator. I provided the investigator with written copies of the stories that were told to me by my daughter. After the DYFS investigator completed her investigation regarding my daughter, the investigator informed me that the actions of my daughter's mother are inappropriate, but her actions are not considered to be abusive. She further stated, "We cannot tell parents how to discipline their children."

Apparently, DYFS does not take into consideration all forms of abuse. As you will see, the issues related to the way my daughter is being handled by her mother warrant the attention and intervention of a child welfare agency (DYFS). Yet, the actions of my daughter's mother which are described below does not rise to the level of child abuse in accordance with the standards utilized by the Division of Youth and Family Services.

Please note, the stories listed below are written in the words of my daughter as she explained the details of these events in writing.

We were at Mount Olive Baptist church on a first Sunday. I did not know any better because I was only seven years old. When the bowl for communion came around with the grape juice and crackers, I took two communion packets and ate the crackers. I thought the crackers were supposed to be eaten as food. When we got home, my mom made me get butt naked and she hit me with her hand for doing what I did at the church.

When I was in the fourth grade, my mom told me I could not participate in the field day events at my elementary school. She had taken away my privileges for some reason that I cannot remember. I did not participate in any events. When field day was over, I was playing catch with some of my friends. That was not a part of the field day events. My mom drove by the school, parked her car and saw me playing catch. She yelled out my name many times until I acknowledged her. When I turned around, she yelled at me to get my stuff and that she was taking me home. I ran upstairs to my classroom in fear of my mom. I got my back pack and I told my teacher I was going home. My teacher seemed concerned. When I got in the car, my mom was yelling at me and asking me why I was playing at the field's day event. I told her field day was over and I was playing because it was over. She continued to yell at me. When we got home she made me go upstairs and get all of my favorite toys.

She made me put each one of my favorite toys in a plastic garbage bag slowly. She said that she wanted me to realize what I was doing to make me feel sadder since she is going to throw my toys in the garbage.

I came back from Hershey Park with my mother. On the day we returned it was my dad's weekend to have me. I told my mother that I wanted to visit with my dad. She got mad at me. She said I did not appreciate the time we had at Hershey Park.

Before my dad was supposed to pick me up, I had to work with my math tutor at the Teaneck, New Jersey library. My mother told me that I could not get in her car and I would have to walk from Hackensack, New Jersey to Teaneck, New Jersey in order to get to the library. I had my overnight bag and my poster paper so I could work on a project at my dad's house. I was walking down the block crying on my way to the library in Teaneck. My mom's car was to the left of me when I was walking, but I did not see her until she shouted out my name. I ran across the street to her and she told me to get my "Ass" in the car. She drove me to the library.

On a Tuesday night, my mom asked me did I have any tests for the week. I said yes. I have a test on Wednesday. She looked at me like I should have told her earlier. Then she gave me a choice. She said do you want your privileges taken away or would you rather have a spanking. I said take away my privileges, but she spanked me and took away my privileges.

Something happened where I did something on the computer that my mom did not like. My mom made me stand up and repeat after her saying "Mommy I am stupid, mommy I am stupid, mommy I am stupid." I had to say that at least five times.

I run track. I was told by mom not to run in the Hollister (expensive clothing). But I did anyway for one track practice. I also uncaringly threw my Hollister sweat jacket on the floor. All of my track team members including me were in a huddle. The coach was telling us where the next track meet was going to be. I got called out of the huddle by my mom just so she could yell at me for wearing the Hollister during track practice. When we got in the car, she hit me in my head with her hand. She had a ring on her finger, and it left a small cut on my forehead above my left eyebrow. Then she told me when we get home that I was getting my ass kicked. While she was telling me that, she was continuously punching me in my arm. When we got home she beat me so hard and I screamed so loud that I was surprised no neighbors rang my doorbell. She left three big whelps on my left leg. When she was done, she made me go upstairs and take a shower. She beat me with a belt for at least a good ten minutes. She held me down while I was on the couch and she continued to hit me.

One day, on Sunday, my mom asked me to clean my room. This was the same Sunday that my dad had just dropped me off. I did not have a problem cleaning my room. Its good to keep things clean. When I was done, I told my mom. She came in to check my room.

She told me I lied because my room was not completely clean, and it was not cleaned to her standards. She hit me with a belt for supposedly lying to her.

I was with my dad for one whole week during spring break. My dad had to drop me off at one of my track meets at 12:30pm. My mom told my dad that 12:30pm would be the right time to drop me off so I could be there in time to prepare for the track meet with my team. When I saw my mother at the stadium with the new clothes I was wearing that my father's wife bought me, my mother asked me where did I get those new clothes from. I told her that I got them while I was with my father. She said to send the clothes back to my father's house. While my dad was on his way to the stadium to see me run track, we ran into each other as I was trying to find him so I could change clothes in his car and put on the clothes that my mother told me to wear. I was crying and I was very upset. When my father saw me, he was very upset about me having to send the clothes back and having to change clothes in his car. He wanted to talk to my mother to find out why she was treating me so badly after she had not seen me for a whole week. I begged my father not to say anything to my mother because I was afraid of her.

We went back to his car and I changed my clothes. When I returned to my mom, she did not let me run track because she said I was late. My father and I arrived at the field at 12:25pm, as she requested. When me and my mother left the track meet, she drove to the bank. I started to get out of the car, but she looked at me like I should not get out of the car. I stayed in the car and she locked the car doors.

Sometime between March and April 2012 my mom was being mean to me and saying that I do not respect myself. She was just being really mean and she was making me cry. She made me so upset that I took my right index finger and I was digging in my skin trying to leave scratch marks because she made me so mad. Little pieces of my skin started to come up off of my hand.

Sometime between the months of January and May 2012, I wore a knitted pink hat with a lid. I had this hat on backwards in the Teaneck library. Later that night, my mom told me to get a black sharpie and some tape. I got it and when I came back she had paper in her hand. She wrote on one paper, "I want to be a boy." On the other paper she wrote, "I want to have a penis." Then she put tape on these papers. She taped one paper to the front of my shirt and she taped the other paper on the back of my shirt and made me walk around the house. Then she sat me down. I was crying and she said that if I wanted to be a boy she would take me to the hospital to get a penis and have my sex changed.

She also said that she was going to send me to school with those papers taped on my shirt. But, the next day I did not have to wear the paper taped on my shirt when I went to school.

On 6/5/12, I was coming from basketball practice. I was in the front seat of my mom's car. I took a quiz that day and I got a 77 (C+) on it. She was not to happy with me. I have three weeks left to the school year. She thinks that I am slacking off because there is only three weeks left to school. That is not the truth. The second page of the quiz I did not know most of the work, so I got some wrong. I told her I got those wrong because I didn't know, but she thought that was my excuse. Then I had a math final exam coming up, and so on a preparation assignment I got about eight or nine questions wrong. When we got in the car, I was in the front seat. At about almost every red light or stop sign that we came upon, she would hit me in my head or wherever her hand landed. Then she started yelling and cursing at me. Then on the way back home, she made the wrong turn. She said to me, "You got me going the wrong Fucking way." Then she was like, "You are worried about someone not being your friend, but you got a 77 on a quiz." Then she said, "Your friends don't give a shit about you." The next day I asked her why she hit me. She replied, "Because if I can't get the common sense through to you using words, then maybe I can beat it into you." This is not the first time she hit me when I was in the front seat. She usually hits me in the face at least five or six times within a time period on the way home. Or she just hits me repeatedly until she feels like stopping.

Later in the month of June 2012, I was on my way to the Orthodontist. I came downstairs with high top sneakers on. My mom said, "You have on high top sneakers in 100 degree weather." Then we went to the Orthodontist. When we left the Orthodontist, my mom started yelling at me. She said my hygiene is like a boy's hygiene. Then she started saying that she thinks I want to be a boy, and how she gave birth to a girl. If I want to be a boy, then get the fuck out of her house and I started crying. Then we went to the bank. She parked her car at the bank. She yelled at me and said, "You are a fucking lesbian. Go find another lesbian and lick her pussy." She tore me apart when she said that. Then when we got back home, she asked me if I like boys or girls, and I answered boys. Then she pretended to call my dad. She made like she was talking to him on the phone. She said, "Keep Taylor for the rest of the summer because I am annoyed with her." She also said, 'Taylor is not a girl. If she wanted to stay in my house, I would have to live by her requirements, and her rules."

Very often my mom calls me a boy. She does not like when I wear high top sneakers. I play basketball and I like to wear high top sneakers. On July 9, 2012, my mom threw away all of my high top sneakers. She did not throw away the high top sneakers my uncle bought me. He is her brother, but she threw away a brand new pair of my high top Adidas that my dad bought me. I suggested that she give the sneakers back to my dad, but she didn't listen to me and she threw the sneakers away.

On another day in July 2012, before my mom threw away my high top sneakers, I came downstairs with high tops and basketball shorts on. She started yelling at me. She was saying that I been wearing high tops to summer camp for two weeks. She wanted to see if I would wear my low cut sneakers.

But she told me I could wear my high tops, she denied that she said that. I had to change sneakers. She told me that if I wanted to be a boy, then I had to get the hell out of her house.

On Saturday, July 21, 2012, I had to take a cup of milk with me to the library. My mother wanted me to drink some milk on this day. After about 45 minutes of being in the library, I came back to her car. My mom told me to drink the milk and it was warm. Then I had to go to basketball practice.

Two hours later when practice ended, my mom made me drink this hot milk on this hot summer day. When my dad came to pick me up later that day, I did not finish the milk. My mom told me that I would have to finish the glass of milk when I came back home on Monday.

On July 23, 2012, I had a field trip planned at my summer day camp. My mom told me to show her what I was wearing for that trip. I showed her my clothes while she was on the phone. When she got off the phone, she took out one of her belts from her dresser drawer, and I got beat with a belt for showing her the clothes I wanted to wear while she was on the phone.

On that same day, five to ten minutes later, I showed my mother the sneakers that I was going to wear on my field trip the next day. We were instructed at camp to wear an old pair of sneakers to the water park for this trip. I found an old scratched up pair of white high top sneakers. My mom beat me with a belt again for choosing a pair of high top sneakers. Then she picked out a pair of low cut sneakers for me to wear on the field trip.

Conclusion of Written Stories from my Daughter's Journal of Abusive Experiences

It was very, very painful for me to record these stories for you to read regarding the abuse that my daughter is experiencing at the hands of her mother. However, I am not sure what is more painful for me. I wonder if it is the abuse that my daughter is experiencing with her mother, or is it the fact that DYFS will not do anything to stop her mother from abusing my daughter. During this period of time, my daughter was 12 years old. She told me that her mother has been treating her in this cruel and unusual fashion since she was five years old. However she just recently started to bring these matters to my attention. The first major report of abuse my daughter shared with me was in January 2010 when her mother put soap in her mouth and spanked her. DYFS took no corrective steps to hold my daughter's mother accountable for her abusive behavior in that case. Now her mother is totally out of control with her abusive behavior.

DYFS has a standard that black and blue marks have to be present on a child's body before they make a determination that child abuse has occurred. Although no marks have been discovered by DYFS on my daughter's body, how much more of this abuse is she suppose to endure before she might run away from home, act out in school, go into a state of depression, and turn out to be an abusive person herself. God forbid if my daughter decides to do something to hurt herself because she cannot get help from the only option available to help her in this matter. The agency that is charged with the responsibility to protect her from an abusive parent makes decisions that protect the abusive parent. The only option my daughter has is "DYFS or Die First."

Who is the Family in Family Court?

What I discuss in this chapter is not an indictment of all judges and other staff related to the family court system. The focus of this story pertains to the specific judges and court personnel I encountered during my experiences as a plaintiff in family court.

I have been involved in a high volume of cases. I probably received court orders from every judge in the family court system located in Hackensack, New Jersey. As a matter of fact, I have been there so many times there are some judges who have presided over my cases more than once.

In addition, all of these judges seemed to have the same traits. They were all white, mean spirited and impatient. It seemed like they even had the same DNA in that they all act and think alike. Every one of those judges handled my cases as if they had heard it all before. The myopic views of these judges regarding my family issues led to poor decision making on their part. The judges refused to look at the issues based on their merit.

In college, I learned in my business law class that every case is different. All legal cases should be dealt with on a case-by-case basis. But in reality, the family court system is a closed system. It is open only to those who work within the framework of the legal process.

After my experiences in family court, I now realize that this is not the place to resolve family issues. Essentially, there is no equal justice, no fairness, no care, no concern, and there is no compassion provided by the judges regarding your family issues. As it stands in many cases, we come to family court already fractured and brokenhearted as a result of the fights with our ex-mates regarding our children. Then we make our way to family court to try and resolve our issues.

In the mind of a reasonable person, a place called family court sounds like a safe place to go. And, unfortunately it is the only forum available for parents to resolve their family issues regarding custody, child support, and other family matters.

The moral of this story is that the real family in family court are the judges, attorneys, law clerks, court officers, and the clerical support staff. This is the group that defines who the family really is in family court.

The judges tend to the needs of the attorneys. The attorneys appease the judges. The court clerks and court officers demonstrate a high level of respect for the attorneys. The attorneys kiss the butts of the court clerks, court officers, and clerical staff to remain in good standing with the judges. All the care and concern they show towards one another comes at the expense of your family. They stand united. They show more love, respect, and compassion for each other than they do for us who need them the most. And we have to pay for their services. Even as adversaries, the attorneys have better relationships with each other than they do with us as their clients. One of the amazing things I have noticed about how the real family in family court operates is how the attorneys play together in a corner just like brothers and sisters. When they do that, they usually cut a deal that their clients did not authorize.

In other words, the attorneys, in theory, are adversaries who represent their respective clients in a court of law. However, quite often, these attorneys meet behind closed doors with the judges. They cut deals that work for them to settle your case. Then they are excited to present their deal to you. The attorneys coerce you into signing a settlement that you neither agreed to nor requested that a deal be made on your behalf. If you disagree with their settlement and refuse to sign, the attorneys tell you to sign it or pay them $10,000 more to fight your case in court at a trial.

At that point, you may find that you have no choice but to sign a deal that you did not have any input regarding the provisions that affect your life, your child and your finances. Eventually, you sign the deal because you have no more money to fight in court. You have already spent the money when you paid the attorney to represent you in the case where he/she cut a deal. After you sign the settlement, the attorneys shake hands. Then you find out that you are in a worse position now than you were before you paid this attorney $3500 to represent you. To exacerbate the situation, at the time when you first met the attorney you were assured that your case stood on solid legal ground. However, once you arrive in court, you find out that what was considered solid legal ground by your attorney is subject to the whims of the good motherly or fatherly judges. During the review of your Motion by the judges, the attorneys do not cite any established case law to advocate your position. Instead, they usually acquiesce to the directives of their mother or father (judge). Subsequently, you as the client get screwed. The attorneys are happy with each other because they did not have to work too hard to earn the $3500 paid to them by their respective clients. In their minds, they did the work of a good family and settled your case in the best interest of the judges schedules.

Further, the attitudes of the judges and court officers are cold and callous. Quite often, I have found that they did not talk to me in a respectful manner. Instead, they yelled and screamed at me, as if I was in criminal court. I have worked for the New York City Department of Corrections. I have visited correctional facilities on Riker's Island in Queens, New York. And, I have to say that there is no difference in the way inmates are treated in these correctional facilities compared to the way fathers are treated in family court. The only difference is that fathers are not shackled with handcuffs in family court. However, fathers are shackled with usurious legal fees, child support, and incarceration if we failed to pay child support in a timely fashion.

Some of the family court judges are mothers and fathers themselves. Yet, they seem to have no idea about the pain and suffering fathers experience before they arrive in their court rooms. We go there for relief. But, all we seem to get is lots of grief.

For some strange reason, the judges act as if good fathers are not good enough to have their issues adjudicated in a fair way.

I am cognizant of the fact that the family court system is a business. It is in the business of handling the issues of our broken families. As fathers, we come to court filled with emotion, pain, and hope. These judges know about the issues we deal with. We have to file a Notice of Motion, which requires us to list our issues and our requests for relief in detail. By the time we get to court, we may not have seen our children for weeks, months, and in some cases, years. These judges know we come to their court rooms broke financially. We cannot afford to pay our child support. And we cannot afford to pay an attorney. These judges see our emotions flare up when we storm out of their courtrooms after another unfair decision.

Yet, the judges treat fathers like we do not hurt. It seems to be annoying to judges that fathers even come to court. Although most of the male judges in the Bergen County family court system have heads full of gray hair, they do not bring any grandparent compassion or wisdom to their courtrooms.

In family court, your issues are never fully addressed. The judges make their decisions based on what they determine to be important from the issues listed in your Notice of Motions. The incomplete decisions we receive from judges do not address all of the issues that were originally presented. Therefore, your case is set up to be recycled. This will ensure that you will return to fight with your ex-mate about the same issues on a different date. True closure is never realized due to these incomplete court cases, which fail to address your issues in a comprehensive fashion.

Therefore, in this process, nobody ever really wins. You spend lots of money. You waste lots of time. You get drained emotionally. It is a true exercise in futility.

Family court is a place where you may have to deal with some cold-hearted court officers, court clerks, law clerks, attorneys, and judges.

It does not feel like a place that is good for family. I assure you that your family is not what really matters in this process. That is because the only family in family court are the people who work there. Consequently, in my never-ending fight with my ex-wife to enforce my parenting rights, I came to learn who the real family is in family court.

When you divorce, when you do not communicate, and you have children in the middle of your fight, you may spend a lot of time in family court. If you do, you will find out that family court has nothing to do with your family. Nor does family court do what is best for your children.

You should not turn your vital family issues over to judges who have no care or concern for your children. It is imperative that you work out your own issues. The court system only cares about the money generated from the issues between you and your ex-mate. Remember, the family court system is a business. It is not a place where you can find support for your family issues.

Before I close on this subject, I would like to recognize the Bergen County Probation Office for the respect they showed me. During the times I have been unemployed, I may have been tardy paying my child support. I would notify my ex-wife to let her know the check was in the mail. However, she would still call the Probation Department to request that a warrant be issued for my arrest.

Fortunately for me, the Probation Department always showed compassion for me and my financial position. They would warn me by telephone that a warrant was pending for my arrest.

As it has turned out, I have not been arrested and/or incarcerated for failing to pay child support. Essentially, the representatives from the Probation Department seemed to understand that I could not make timely child support payments because I was unemployed.

Finally, the family court legal system is not conducive to representing the best interests of your family. It does not operate in the spirit of resolving sensitive family issues. The name of a place called family court can be misleading. And, it can be disheartening to see how those who work in that system take good care of each other. And at the same time, they have no regard for you and your family.

During my time spent in family court, I have seen no compassion from any of the judges that I have stood before. The family court judges seem to not really give a damn. There has been no concern about what has happened between me and my ex-wife regarding my quest to spend time with my daughter.

Instead, the judges in family court placed more value on me not having an attorney than it did to support my rights to spend time with my daughter. If the purpose of family court is to do what is in the best interest of the children, then family court has failed miserably in my case.

I have learned that the only relief you may find in family court is to know your family is not the focus. There is no care utilized in the adjudication of your very important family issues regarding your children. But the family in family court will remain strong, happy, and financially intact!

If you are new to the family court process, do not look for any hugs from the judges no matter how bad you think your rights have been violated by your ex-mate. Your case is just another case in the hopper. You should expect to be handled like any other case on the docket.

The Criminal Elements of Family Court

On the pages that follow, I will take you on a journey to the place known as family court. I want to share my story with you as to how I came to discover "The criminal elements of family court."

When I look back over the years, I am amazed that I have been to family court so many times to enforce my parental rights. What I have found to be most amazing is that instead of having my parenting rights enforced, I have been ripped off financially, robbed of my parenting time, deceived by judges, misled by attorneys, and mugged by a court appointed Family Mediator. Further, and most importantly, I have been denied equal justice under the law due to the political bias and capricious decisions of these judges.

When I think about the way this clandestine activity was carried out by these agents of family court, it is clear that their behavior reeks of criminal activity. The arrogance of the judges, attorneys, and Family Mediators is propelled by their belief that there is no authority available to hold them accountable. Their criminal activity begins and ends with them, and there is no place for the average person to go for help.

For instance, what would the police do if I reported that I was robbed of money by a family court judge? What would an attorney do if I wanted to utilize their services to hold a judge accountable for abuse and misuse of his/her authority?

One of my first experiences of being mugged in family court came at the hands of a family mediator. During one of the many battles I had with the ex-wife in family court, a judge ordered that our case be referred to a family mediator. In the court's eyes, the use of a family mediator is considered to be a more effective method of addressing ongoing unresolved post marital issues. Accordingly, our case was assigned for us to work with a court-ordered family mediator.

The person designated to handle our case charged a retainer fee of $2,000. Her retainer fee had to be split by me and the ex-wife. We both had to pay 50% each of the family mediator's retainer fee. In other words, we were both required to pay her $1,000 each. At that time, I was financially challenged.

I worked per diem as a human resources consultant, and I collected unemployment benefits. I could not afford the family mediator's fee. Based on my other pressing financial obligations, this was a very stressful time for me financially.

To make matters worse, the mediator pressed me for her money. Eventually, she reported me to the judge. She cited me for not cooperating with her. However, on numerous occasions, I had advised the mediator that I just could not afford to pay her fee.

Consequently, I was fined by the judge to pay $500 for not cooperating with the family mediator.

Two years later

In another case in family court against my ex-wife, my attorney advised me that I had been overcharged by the family mediator. The attorney said family mediators have the option to modify their fee schedule in cases of financial hardship.

In the scenario above, the family mediator did not offer me any options for a modified fee. Instead, she offered me an installment payment plan to pay her fee in full. Subsequently, I had to pay the full amount of her fee in addition to the $500 fine.

If you spend enough time in the family court system, you will see how the judges keep these cases going. As previously noted, the court orders issued by these judges do not fully address the issues presented for resolution. Consequently, you will find yourself returning to family court a second and third time to address issues that were not resolved in your first application to the court for relief.

In addition, for some strange reason, the mothers of our children tend to come out on the winning side in most of these cases. It seems like they do not have to prove what they allege in court. This lack of fair play also helps to keep fathers tied up in family court. We keep going back to fight for our so-called father's rights that are mysteriously not enforced by the judges in family court.

In another dispute with the ex-wife in family court, the judge added a change in his written court order that was not discussed in court. He included a provision which stated that I do not discuss any marital issues with my daughter.

On that day in court, my ex-wife and I disagreed about a variety of issues. However, none of those issues dealt with discussions that I had with our daughter. As a matter of fact, that issue has never been on the table in any of the cases that I have been involved with in family court regarding the ex-wife.

At the end of this hearing, I remember the judge verbally stated what his decisions were regarding the issues presented. The judge adjourned the case. As he departed from the courtroom, he stated that he would return to his chambers to complete his decision in writing. He further stated that we would receive copies of his decision in the mail.

When I received my copy of his court order, I noticed that the judge included a provision which stated that I should not discuss any marital issues with my daughter. I was taken aback by the inclusion of this provision. In my mind, it reeked of foul play. If that provision was not discussed in court, then it should not have been ordered by the judge that I comply with his ruling on that issue.

And since the case had been adjourned, I left the courtroom. As I was leaving, I noticed that my ex-wife's attorney remained in the courtroom. I thought for a moment that I should wait too. However, I had to catch a bus to New York City. I had to make my way to work.

In my absence, it appears that her attorney met with the judge. Apparently, they discussed the inclusion of that provision. And arbitrarily, the judge included that provision as part of his written court order.

In the next case, you will see that this judge committed a crime of robbery in the first degree. I appeared in court to respond to a Notice of Motion filed by the ex-wife. She was seeking an increase in child support. I represented myself (Pro se) in this case.

At the time my ex-wife filed for this increase in child support, she earned $160,000 per year. In addition, she earned a five-figure annual salary bonus. On the other hand, I earned $85,000 per year.

On this day in court, the judge informed her attorney that based on her salary, she would only be entitled to a $33 per month increase. This slight increase would bump up my child support payment to approximately $267 every other week.

When she heard that, I could see the disappointment on her face. Her plan to set me back financially seemingly failed. The judge advised her attorney to see if she wanted to proceed with her claim. This time around, an increase based on the New Jersey child support guidelines did not seem like a good deal. However, she decided to accept the increase. And the increase was ordered by the judge. The case was adjourned.

Just like in the previous case, the judge did not provide us with a copy of his order. He said his decision would be mailed to both parties. I said to myself, "Do not leave the courtroom." I remembered what happened in the previous case.

The judge included a provision in his order that was not discussed in court. At the conclusion of this case, my ex-wife's attorney did not leave the courtroom. However, once again, I was pressed for time. I had to make it back to my office in New York City. I left the courtroom.

One week later, I received the judge's court order. I was shocked. The $33 increase in child support was not stipulated in the court order. Instead, there was a $200 increase in child support. This increase was based on "Child care" for my daughter after school. Based on my ex-wife's salary, the New Jersey child support guidelines did not provide for a satisfactory increase to her liking. Once again, in my absence, her attorney and the judge manipulated their legal system and manufactured this increase.

Not only was this increase illegal, but also the method in which the $200 increase was devised went against our divorce settlement agreement. In the settlement agreement between us issued at the time of our divorce, it clearly states in pertinent part, ". . . if the father pays child support . . . child care is the sole and exclusive responsibility of the mother . . ."

Therefore, I should not be subjected to an increase in child support as it relates to child care. Based on the fact that this judge breached my divorce settlement agreement with his decision, I had to hire an attorney to file a motion to request that the judge reconsider his court order.

According to the attorney I hired to represent me in this case, the law provides that an individual has thirty days to request a judge to reconsider their decision. I vehemently disagreed with the judge's decision. As a result of this clandestine activity between the judge and her attorney, I had to pay an additional $200 in child support. In addition, I had to pay an attorney $2,500 to undo this criminal act. At that time, my ex-wife earned $75,000 more than me. In addition to her bonuses which exceeded $25,000 a year. Why would family court stick me up for $200 in child care which I was not required to pay?

When I first met with my attorney about this case, she assured me that the judge's decision was inappropriate. Based on my divorce settlement agreement, the attorney cited every relevant section of family law that could be utilized to support my case. In addition, my attorney told me that the judge did this because I represented myself.

The attorney said, "Judges do not respect people who go Pro se."

She further stated, "The judge saw you as a *scofflaw* (a contemptuous law violator)."

If that was the judge's perception of me, that would be another illegal act on the part of this judge. That would be a violation of my civil rights. The judge discriminated against me. In this case, all I did was file the appropriate papers.

For the record, I am an educated (Master's degree) taxpaying American citizen. I do not have a criminal record. I do not have any traffic violations on my record. How could I be so disrespected by a judge? Although the ex-wife did not have any legal basis for a $200 increase in child support, I had no chance to win because the judge saw me as a scofflaw.

I utilized a process to represent myself which was created by the court system. This process says I have a right to represent myself. Yet the judges who preside over these cases frown upon their own system. Hmmm . . .

After meeting with my attorney, I was excited about going back to court. I had high hopes that the judge would reverse his decision.

However, on the day we went to court, I never saw the judge. My attorney and the attorney who represented the ex-wife met with the judge behind closed doors. At the conclusion of their meeting, my attorney told me that the judge said I was right. I should not have to pay a $200 increase in child support related to child care.

Then my attorney advised me that the judge also said that he is not going to change his decision. The attorney informed me that she worked out a deal. The attorney said, "Your ex-wife would not be able to seek another increase in child support for an entire year."

I told the attorney that another increase in child support is not my issue. My issue is that she was awarded a $200 increase in child support that she is not entitled to receive.

My attorney said, "Mr. Gardner, you could accept this agreement. Or you can pay me another $5,000 to $10,000 to go to trial and see if the judge might reconsider changing his decision. As far as this case is concerned, the judge said he is not going to change his decision, unless you file a new motion requesting that he do so."

As you can see, I was robbed. The judge said I was right about the wrong decision that he made. I hired an attorney to file the paperwork within the specified time required. But the judge refused to change his decision. It did not matter that I followed the court guidelines to the letter of the law. I hired an attorney to eradicate the judge's fictitious image of me as a scofflaw. Need I say anything more about the criminal element of family court?

I would like to stop here, except I have a few more examples of this criminal activity. During the times I have represented myself in court, I noticed some other inappropriate actions between the ex-wife's attorney and the judges. I have seen my ex-wife's attorney go in and out of the judge's chambers.

The issue here is that we are involved in an adversarial legal proceeding. The judge serves as the supposedly neutral third party. I am the plaintiff. She is the defendant. We are considered adversaries seeking relief for our issues. The neutral third party is not supposed to meet with either side, unless both parties are represented.

In labor law, major contractual and disciplinary issues between Management and Labor Unions are addressed at arbitration hearings. These hearings are presided over by arbitrators. An arbitrator is a neutral third party who functions in the same fashion as a judge in family court. An arbitrator would not discuss an issue with management unless there is a representative from the union present.

The same is true for unemployment hearings. An Administrative Law Judge would not speak to the employer at an unemployment hearing unless the former employee is present.

Those are prime examples of the role regarding a neutral third party in adversarial proceedings. The process is exactly the same in a court of law.

If a judge meets with one party in the absence of the other, it would severely compromise their position of neutrality. In addition, it would provide an unfair advantage to one party over the other. In the cases above, the judges not only compromised their neutrality, but also they undermined the law which they are appointed to uphold. This capricious activity subjected my cases to despotic behavior on the part of these judges. If this is not criminal, it is certainly grossly inappropriate.

To date, the biggest crime I experienced in family court was when the judge robbed me of my parenting time. This case is well documented in chapter 3, "Evidence of Access Denied."

Here is a quick review of the details regarding that case. I initiated a claim in family court to have my parenting rights enforced. The ex-wife interfered with my visitation for five consecutive months. She retaliated against me for a complaint I made to DYFS regarding her abusive behavior toward our daughter.

In her own defense, she claimed my daughter did not want to spend any time with me. Then the judge seemed to view this matter as a case of my word against her word. To get to the bottom of this issue, the judge interviewed our daughter.

After his investigation, the judge informed us that my daughter definitely wants to be with me. He said there is no doubt in his mind that everything is alright with me and my daughter.

However, the judge said he decided not to reinstate my overnight parenting time. His rationale was that my daughter should slowly readjust to staying overnight with me.

The judge reduced my parenting time to one Saturday every other weekend. The judge did not sanction the ex-wife for the five months she interfered with my parenting time.

In that situation, I tried to enforce my parenting rights. Based on the lack of evidence provided by the ex-wife in this particular case, it was very clear that this woman violated my rights as a father, yet she experienced no consequences, and I ended up with practically no quality parenting time.

The judge applied his unsaid and unwritten rules to diminish me as a father in the life of my daughter.

Not once did the judge consider the importance and significance of my role as a father in my daughter's life. Instead, it was more important to the judge and my ex-wife's attorney to manipulate their legal system, and collaborate on an agreement that stripped my parenting time down to the bone. Yet, family court is a legal system which maintains that the premise for all of their decisions is based on what is in the best interest of the child. Hmmm . . .

In that case, the judge conspired with the defendant's attorney and kidnapped my daughter. In the United States of America, kidnapping is a crime!

Devalued by the Law

On or about July 5, 2005, I was scheduled to appear in family court based on another summons initiated by the ex-wife. She wanted me to pay not only my current child support due, but also my child support that was in arrears.

As previously noted, I worked as a human resources consultant. As an HR consultant, I was not assigned work on a consistent basis. Consequently, I could not afford to pay my child support.

I fell behind by $3,000. In addition, this summons was a part of a more sinister plan being executed by the ex-wife to ruin me financially. My father use to say, "The best time to kick a man is when he's down."

Based on my employment status, and my inability to pay my bills, my ex-wife knew it would be easy to execute her plan. She kicked me hard to make sure I stayed down.

In addition, the spring and summer of 2005 was a very tough time for me. Compounded with my financial problems, I had far more significant challenges trying to pay for my life-sustaining medications. I had no health benefits at that time. I am a type 1 diabetic with hypertension. My insulin costs $100 for one vial. I used two types of insulin. The second vial of insulin cost $70. The syringes I use to inject my insulin cost $100 per box.

I also take two types of blood pressure medicine. The medicine I take in the morning cost $90 for one thirty-day prescription. The medicine I take at night cost $55 for the second thirty-day prescription. As a matter of fact, all of my prescriptions had to be refilled every thirty days. With no health benefits, and an urgent need to sustain my life with my required medications, I had to pay out of pocket to refill my prescriptions. Therefore, I had to borrow lots of money.

In two words, I was in "Financial Hell." I was stressed. I was depressed. I was always in a fight with the ex-wife. All of this was going on when I received the summons to appear in court on July 5, 2005. If I did not have the support of my current wife, who was my girlfriend at the time, I am not sure how I would have made it through those gut-wrenching times.

Now, let's go back to the day I was devalued by the law in family court at the child support hearing. When I arrived in court, I noticed the hearing officer was an African American woman. At that moment, I felt good about my case. I thought an African American hearing officer would be good for my situation. I am an African American. I really thought this woman would understand my plight.

The second thing I noticed was that the ex-wife was not in court that day. Instead, her oldest brother appeared on her behalf while she vacationed in the Bahamas. With her absence, I thought this would be a good day for me in court.

When the case began, the hearing officer asked me why I did not pay child support. I explained to the hearing officer that when I worked full-time, I paid child support as scheduled. However, based on my current status, I could not afford to pay child support.

I also explained to the hearing officer that I did not have any health benefits. I told her that I am a diabetic with hypertension. I went on to explain that my medications are very expensive, and without my medication, I could not sustain my own life.

I further explained to the hearing officer that with all of my other living expenses, I have to pay out of pocket for my medication and medical supplies. I also provided the hearing officer with a breakdown regarding the cost of my medications. I thought the hearing officer would understand that I was in a very, very difficult position financially.

To my surprise, the hearing officer yelled at me.

She said, "I don't care! You are required to pay child support for your daughter. And you could have paid $5 a week to show some effort."

She continued to yell at me when she said, "You will pay your child support. If you fail to do so, a warrant will be issued for your arrest."

Then she signed the court order that required me to resume my biweekly child support payments. In addition, her court order required me to pay the child support in arrears of $3,000. I had to make three lump sum payments within a three-month period. I cried like a baby when she handed me her court order. Then she called for her next case.

As I left the court building, my ex-wife's brother caught up with me on the street. He told me that he had no idea I was struggling to pay for my medicine. Then he hugged me. I told him that I was devastated by the decision of the hearing officer.

On this day, I was absolutely astounded by the way I was treated. I could not believe this hearing officer showed total disdain for my life. I wondered how a law-abiding, and taxpaying citizen could be so devalued by the law. I had not committed any crime. I was not on trial for murder. I pleaded to the court that I could not afford my medications to sustain my own life. Should I allow myself to die in order to pay child support?

Throughout my adult life I have worked hard. And, I pay my taxes. Up until the point where I fell on some difficult times I paid my child support in a timely fashion. I graduated from college. I completed my graduate school education.

However, on this day in family court, none of that mattered. The only option this hearing officer gave me was to pay child support and die. Or do not pay child support and go to jail.

For the record, the ex-wife would not have accepted $5 a week from me as a child support payment. I did communicate with her regarding the fact that I could not pay my child support in a timely manner. She disregarded my circumstances and dragged me back into court. I told the hearing officer that my ex-wife earned more than $100,000 in salary on an annual basis.

The hearing officer said, "That is not the point, you are supposed to pay your child support!"

I was totally demoralized. It was hard to understand why a person in a position of authority would have no regard for me as a human being.

My insulin and hypertension medications sustain my life. Without my medications, there would be no chance for me to pay child support. The people who administer the child support laws in family court had no concerns regarding my life. The hearing officer did not care for me as a human being. I am a worthy person who experienced some very tough financial times.

This was the first time in my life that I had ever been close to financial ruin. Yet in a family court in the state of New Jersey, I was totally devalued by the law. I could not meet my financial obligations. What crime did I commit? I had to pay for my medications to sustain my life so one day I would be able to resume my child support payments.

Your Children as PODs

Prisoners of Divorce

Throughout this book you have read stories about my experiences with child pawn and its negative effects, as it relates to my daughter. You have also learned about the devastating experiences of others who shared their stories with you about the perils of child pawn. At this point, my hope is that you have been enlightened regarding the extensive emotional and mental health damage that this type of activity can have on the lives of your children.

In this chapter, I have provided some additional information for you. This information comes from mental health professionals who are experts on the subject regarding the emotional health of children when they are used as pawns.

Further, this information will broaden your perspective on this subject. It will provide additional insight that will give you some guidance as to how to deal with these experiences. Hopefully, you will never cross that bridge. However, if not you, there will be somebody that you know who will experience these challenges with an ex-mate and their children. Perhaps, now you will be in a better position to shed some light on this subject for the person you know that may dealing with the horrors of child pawn.

Love and Stockholm Syndrome:

The Mystery of Loving an Abuser

By Joseph M. Carver, PhD (Excerpts of his findings outlined below)

On August 23, 1973, two machine gun-carrying criminals entered a bank in Stockholm Sweden.

Blasting their guns, a prison escapee named Jan-Erik Olsson announced to the terrified bank employees, "The party has just begun!"

The two bank robbers held four hostages, three women and one man, for the next one hundred thirty-one hours. The hostages were strapped with dynamite and held in a bank vault until finally rescued on August 28.

After their rescue, the hostages exhibited a shocking attitude considering they were threatened, abused, and feared for their lives for over five days.

In their media interviews, it was clear that they supported their captors and actually feared law enforcement personnel who came to their rescue. The hostages had begun to feel the captors were actually protecting them from the police.

One woman later became engaged to one of the criminals and another developed a legal defense fund to aid in their criminal defense fees. Clearly, the hostages had "bonded" emotionally with their captors.

While the psychological condition in hostage situations became known as Stockholm Syndrome due to the publicity, the emotional bonding with captors was a familiar story in psychology. It had been recognized many years before and was found in studies of other hostage, prisoner, or abusive situations such as:

- Abused Children
- Battered/Abused Women
- Prisoners of War
- Cult Members
- Incest Victims

- Criminal Hostage Situations
- Concentration Camp Prisoners
- Controlling/Intimidating Relationships

In the final analysis, emotionally bonding with an abuser is actually a strategy for survival for victims of abuse and intimidation. The "Stockholm syndrome" reaction in hostage and/or abuse situations is so well recognized at this time that police hostage negotiators no longer view it as unusual.

In fact, it is often encouraged in crime situations as it improves the chances for survival of the hostages. On the down side, it also assures that the hostages experiencing Stockholm syndrome will not be very cooperative during rescue or criminal prosecution.

Stockholm Syndrome (SS) can also be found in family, romantic, and interpersonal relationships. The abuser may be a husband or wife, boyfriend or girlfriend, father or mother, or any other role in which the abuser is in a position of control and authority.[1]

For those of you who may have experienced your children or other loved ones supporting their abusers, hopefully the information above will provide a foundation for understanding how and why the abused support their abuser.

---

1   1. Dr. Carver, Joseph M. Love and Stockholm Syndrome: The Mystery of Loving an Abuser. www.mental-helath-matters.com. 2010-06-30. URL:http://www. mental-health-matters.com. Accessed: 2010-06-30. (*Archived by WebCite* at *http:// www.webcitation.org/5qsKUynfP*).

Parental Alienation
Syndrome and Your Child

What Is Parental Alienation Syndrome?

The definition of PAS as described by Richard A. Gardner who discovered the syndrome and has become an expert in dealing with the issue:

> The parental alienation syndrome (PAS) is a disorder that arises primarily in the context of child-custody disputes. Its primary manifestation is the child's campaign of denigration against a parent, a campaign that has no justification. It results from the combination of a programming (brainwashing) parent's indoctrinations and the child's own contributions to the vilification of the target parent.

(Excerpted from: Gardner, R. A. (1998). The Parental Alienation Syndrome, Second Edition, Cresskill, NJ: Creative Therapeutics Inc.)

Basically, this means that through verbal and nonverbal thoughts, actions and mannerisms, a child is emotionally abused—brainwashed—into thinking the other parent is the enemy. This ranges from bad mouthing the other parent in front of the children, to withholding visits, to pre-arranging the activities for the children while visiting with the other parent.[2]

When your child custody battles have been resolved, you should seriously consider the services of a mental health professional to work with your children. This type of intervention is highly recommended in order to replenish the emotional health of your children. In addition, mental health services for both you and your children will facilitate the process to rebuild a loving relationship between you and your abused children.

---

2   2. Gardner, Richard A. What is Parental Alienation Syndrome (PAS)?. Internet and book excerpts from, "The Parental Alienation Syndrome" 2010-06-30. URL:http://www.paskids.com. Accessed: 2010-06-30. HYPERLINK "http://www. webcitation.org/5qsMIa7FM" *(Archived by WebCite® at http://www.webcitation. org/5qsMIa7FM)*

Problems suffered by children due to the effects of Parental Alienation Syndrome

By Ludwig F. Lowenstein, PhD, Southern England Psychological Services

Justice of the Peace, Vol. 166 No. 24, 2002, p. 464-466

General aspects of children suffering from the effects of PAS

The effect of PAS has been investigated by relatively few individuals so far but I would like to acknowledge my own gratitude to one researcher, Professor Richard A. Gardner for the work he has done in this area. (Gardner 1992, 1998, 2001.) In what follows, we will be concentrating on the effect both short term and long term of parental alienation on children. Whatever one may think children associated with parental alienation are victims but not of their own making.

Parents are responsible for the child becoming a victim and most especially the parent who is carrying out the alienation process. However we will not consider the role of the parent extensively although it must be remembered that they have an important role to play producing the product of alienation.

We will instead concentrate on the child and what his victimization produces. We hear a great deal about child abuse increasingly so especially sexual abuse. We hear somewhat less about emotional abuse. Parental alienation is a form of child abuse since children are being used for the purpose of parents showing their animosity towards the other half of a relationship. The animosity displayed toward the other parent who is being alienated can have a terrible affect on the child in question. Later my own research in this area will be presented indicating the effect upon the child of the alienation process. I will further consider how I feel the problem could best be remedied.

Perhaps the most interesting scenario that occurs is when the child realizes what the alienating or programming parent has been doing and eventually turns against that parent. They often seek the target parent feeling a great sense of guilt in having been a party, albeit an unwilling party, to the humiliation and harm done to the target parent who has done nothing wrong to them to deserve such treatment.

Specific Problems of Children suffering from the Effects of PAS

Now follows a series of symptoms found in children, when they are presented over a period of time with brain washing or programming against another parent. The effects are both short and long term. It must be stated from the beginning that not all the symptoms about to be mentioned occur in all children who are involved in the parental alienation syndrome scenario. There will also be some difference between the very young child and the older child who has more experience with the PAS process. Not all the symptoms mentioned occur in all children. However some symptoms undoutebly will occur and effect the child unless some form of treatment is carried out which eliminates the impact of the alienating process:

1. Anger is a common reaction of many children to the process of alienation. The anger however will be expressed towards the target parent as one sides with one of the parents in the relationship against the other. The fact that the children are forced into this kind of situation causes considerable distress and frustration and the response often is to show aggressive behavior towards the targeted parent in order to accommodate the programmer.
2. Loss or a lack of impulse control in conduct. Children who suffer from PAS are not merely suffering from aggression, but also often turn to delinquent behavior. There is considerable evidence that fathers and their presence and influence can do much to prevent and alleviate the possibility of delinquency most especially in boys.
3. Loss of self-confidence and self-esteem. Losing one of the parents through the programming procedure can produce a lack of self-confidence and self-esteem.
4. Clinging and separation anxiety. Children, especially very young children who have been programmed to hate or disdain one of the parents will tend to cling to that parent who has carried out the programming. There is considerable anxiety induced by the programming parent against the target parent including threats that such a parent would carry out a great number of different negative actions against the child as well as the programming parent.
5. Developing fears and phobias. Many children fear being abandoned or rejected now that they have been induced to feel that one of the partners in a relationship usually the father is less than desirable. Sometimes this results in school phobia that is fear of attending school mainly due to fear

of leaving the parent who claims to be the sole beneficial partner in the formal relationship. Some children suffer from hyperchondriacal disorders and tend to develop psychological symptoms and physical illnesses. Such children also fear what will happen in the future and most especially there is a fear that the programming parent or only parent who is allegedly the "good parent" may die and leave the child bereft of any support.

6. Depression and suicidal ideation. Some children who are so unhappy at the tragic breakup of the relationship are further faced with animosity between the programming parent and the targeted parent. This leads to ambivalence and uncertainty and sometimes suicidal attempts occur due to the unhappiness which the child feels brought about by the two main adults in his or her life.

7. Sleep disorders is another symptom which follows the parental alienation situation. Children frequently dream and often find it difficult to sleep due to their worries about the danger of the alienated parent and the guilt they may feel as a result of participating in the process of alienation.

8. Eating disorders. A variety of eating disorders have been noted in children who are surrounded by parental alienation. This includes anorexia nervosa, obesity and bulima.

9. Educational problems. Children who are surrounded by the pressure of having to reject one parent having been brainwashed frequently suffer from school dysfunctions. They may become disruptive as well as aggressive within that system.

10. Enuresis and Encopresis. A number of very young children due to the pressure and frustrations around them suffer from bed-wetting and soiling. This is a response to the psychological disturbance of losing one parent and finding one parent inimical to the rejected parent.

11. Drug abuse and self destructive behavior frequently are present in children who have suffered from parental alienation. This tendency is due to a need to escape one's feelings of the abuse they have suffered through the experience and the desire to escape from it. In the extreme such self destructive behaviour can lead to suicidal tendencies.

12. Obsessive-compulsive behavior. This psychological reaction is frequently present in PAS children. Such children will seek to find security in their environment by adopting a variety of obsessive compulsive behaviour patterns.

13. Anxiety and panic attacks are also frequently present in children who have been involved in the PAS process. This may be reflected through psycho-somatic disorders such as nightmares.

14. Damaged sexual identity problems. As a result of the PAS syndrome, children often develop identity problems especially as they may have failed to identify with one member of the originally secure relationship.
15. Poor peer relationships may follow the PAS situation due to the fact that such children often are either very withdrawn in their behavior or are aggressive.
16. Excessive feelings of guilt. This may be due to the knowledge deep down that the ostracized parent who has been vilified has done nothing wrong to deserve the kind of treatment received by the child or children. When this view occurs, the child especially when older begins to suffer from guilt feelings.[3]

When and if you decide to alienate your children from the other parent, you may or may not achieve your goal to hurt your ex-mate.

However, your actions will definitely have an adverse impact on the lives of your own children in a significantly negative fashion. These are the children that you have been trusted with to have full responsibility regarding their care and well being. Leave your ex-mate alone and stop destroying your own children!

As with every negative situation, there is a positive solution. The issues related to parental alienation syndrome are very, very serious. However, Dr. Ludwig F. Lowenstein's work above identifies the many issues that can arise as a result of this syndrome. He also provides some tips, which are outlined below as to how to counteract the effects of PAS.

Excerpts of his findings are outlined below.

Signs of Parental Alienation Syndrome

and How to Counteract its Effects

There is no easy way to combat alienation especially if it has taken place for a long period of time and the alienated parent has had little contact with the child. One might say the alienator has won and has complete control of the

---

3   3. Lowenstein PhD, Ludwig F. Problems suffered by children due to the effects of Parental Alienation Syndrome. Southern England Psychological Services. 2010-07-20. URL:http://www.parental-alienation.info/publications. Accessed: 2010-07-20. *(Archived by WebCite® at http://www.webcitation.org/5rMtuXn9I)*

child in this scenario. Both the alienator and the child are a "team" who work totally against the alienated parent for the purpose of humiliating and rejecting that parent from having contact with the victimized child.

Some of the methods that are recommended for dealing with the process of alienation may seem extreme, but it is an extreme situation that one is facing when dealing with the overwhelming power of the alienator.

Typical therapeutic methods are ineffective when dealing with such problems. Very firm approaches are required, and these must be backed unequivocally by the court in order for them to have the effect in debriefing the child, the victim of the alienation.

This sometimes places the therapist in a dangerous situation, for he or she may be accused of being too firm in seeking to reverse the alienation effects. A combination of both reason and emotion, but most of all, firmness must be shown to the child to make them aware of the damage that has been and is being done by continuing to live with such a negative attitude toward one parent. This is, of course, assuming that the alienated parent is innocent of all physical, sexual, or emotional abuse. Below, there is a list of specific steps that you can take to counteract the effects of Parental Alienation Syndrome on your children.

1. Destroy the effects of denigration by one parent toward the other by making the child aware of the happy history before the acrimony and separation between the parents occurred.
2. Get the child to see the good points about the denigrated parent.
3. Be firm and proactive in changing attitudes and behavior that have caused the parental alienation.
4. Appeal to the child's conscience that he or she is rejecting, hurting, and humiliating an innocent party who cares for that child.
5. Warn the parent who alienates the child of the harm that they are doing to the child not just in the present time but in the future also.
6. Appeal to the child's critical thinking—intelligence and emotions—and make the child aware of the unfairness and cruelty in rejecting a loving parent.
7. Make the child aware that they may lose a good parent if the process of alienation continues.
8. Curtail or eliminate telephone calls and other communications from the programming parent while the child is with the noncustodial parent.
9. It is important for children who have been alienated to spend as much time as is possible with the alienated parent alone so that a relationship

can redevelop between them. The longer this individual contact occurs, the greater the likelihood that the alienation process will be depleted.

10. Curtail the child being used as a spy against the alienated parent.

11. It should be remembered that the child who has been the victim of brainwashing needs to know that it is safe to be with the alienated parent without this reducing their loyalty and commitment to the other parent. Hence, the alienated parent should do as much as possible to reassure the child that there is no desire to separate the child from their other parent.

12. Alienated parents, once they have contacted their children, should concentrate on talking about the past and the happy times together, supplemented with pictures or videos. Initially a child could be very offhand and even fail to have eye contact but this can be reduced through reminders of happier times in the past and how this can continue in the future.

13. Alienated parents should not give up easily but should persevere in their efforts to make and maintain contact with their child. Constant rejection from the child is likely to be humiliating and demoralizing, but persistence leads to success with the help of the courts.

It is important to realize that there is a great difference between therapeutic approaches in the normal sense and those that are required with parents who are alienating a child against another parent. It cannot be emphasized too strongly that without the backing of the courts the efforts of the expert involved are unlikely to be effective.[4]

In closing on this subject, please be reminded, based on the research provided above, the idea of using your children as pawns can damage your children emotionally and mentally for life.

It has also been determined that using your children in this manner is considered child abuse. Therefore, any parent who participates in this type of activity should cease and desist immediately from carrying out this abuse on their children. It is against the law to abuse children.

---

4   4. Lowenstein PhD, Ludwig F. Problems suffered by children due to the effects of Parental Alienation Syndrome. Southern England Psychological Services. 2010-07-20. URL:http://www.parental-alienation.info/publications. Accessed: 2010-07-20. (*Archived by WebCite® at http://www.webcitation.org/5rMtuXn9I*)

Therefore, to facilitate your ability to make adjustments and address your needs to help you refrain from this type of behavior toward your ex-mate, I would ask you to turn the page and go to "The Let-Go Lab."

This is the place where you can begin to look at your issues which may cause you to behave in a way that can be totally contrary to both the emotional and mental health of your children. My hope is that after your time spent in the Let-Go Lab, you will begin to address your own emotional health deficits. Thus when you feel good about yourself, it becomes so much easier to be good to someone else.

The Let-Go Lab

Welcome to the "Let-Go Lab." This is the place where you and your ex-mate can come to if you are the angry mother or the sad father, or vice versa. If your anger and sadness are derived from your never-ending bouts with your ex-mate regarding the children, then you are in the right place.

This is where you can find healing for your pain. This is the place where you can learn how to let go. You can learn about the benefits of letting go of bad memories, bad experiences, and bad people. You can also learn how to deal with the emotions created by your volatile, dysfunctional post-relationship issues with your ex-mate.

To solidify the caliber of the exercises in this lab, I collaborated with my good friend and colleague, Dr. Kenneth B. Ballard. He is a relationship expert. Dr. Ballard developed the tools in this lab to provide you with a more effective way to handle relations with yourself and your ex-mate. It is our hope that we meet you where you are in your sadness, madness, and in some cases, your craziness. Our goal is to convert your negative energy into happiness. We want you to find healing and happiness not only for today, but also for tomorrow.

In order for us to do that, there are some things you will have to do. Some of these things may or may not be easy for you. We believe you are very capable and willing to move forward in the right direction. If you read this book, there should be plenty of motivation for you to change the way you handle your business with your ex-mate. In doing so, you will take the first steps required to evolve into a better state of emotional health for yourself. We ask that you please disconnect from your ego.

We ask that you disassociate yourself from the idea of you winning anything and your ex-mate losing everything. For what you are going to do now, everybody wins if you complete your work in the Let-Go Lab.

Therefore, detach yourself from the bad energy of your emotions regarding anger or sadness with your ex-mate. To truly benefit from the exercises in this lab, you have to be willing to separate yourself from things that keep you locked into bad energy. You have to free yourself to make room for the good energy of happiness.

Then you have to take hold of yourself. Control your emotions every day. Purge yourself of the negative energy you have toward your ex-mate. This will make it easier to transition into a space where you can find peace of mind. If you can find peace of mind, you can find happiness on a consistent basis.

On the pages that follow, there will be a variety of exercises combined with a narrative to walk you through your journey to find a better emotional state of mind. We hope that these tools facilitate the transformation of your anger, sadness, and madness into happiness.

Are you ready to change your life today so you can make a better life for yourself tomorrow?

Right now, you hold the key to open the door to the Let-Go Lab. All you have to do is turn the page.

Improve your Emotional Health

Throughout this book, I have stressed the importance of having good emotional health as it relates to children. As adults, it is imperative that our emotional health be intact, as well. If not, after a failed relationship, you may find yourself acting as the person who denies the other parent access to the children.

Good emotional heath has everything to do with anything regarding the way you feel about yourself. If you feel good, you will be good to others.

We all have issues that reside in our past. When we deal with those issues, we can free ourselves to enjoy an emotionally happier and healthier life. If you feel bad because you are unhappy about past experiences in your life, you may stifle your ability to be good to others. Your bad feelings about yourself can lead to dysfunctional relationships with other people on a variety of levels. Therefore, the first step to address bad experiences regarding post relationship issues is to improve your emotional health.

How do you know if you are emotionally healthy? What characteristics do you believe are required to be emotionally healthy?

There are some very important areas you should explore to determine your level of emotional health. You do that by first taking an assessment of your past traumatic experiences regarding child abuse, sexual abuse, rape, and previous relationships. And, you also want to explore any other major issues you have experienced in your life. Such issues, without proper assessment, may impede your ability to be emotionally healthy.

1. Please make an inventory list below of your past traumas, relationships, and other major issues that you have experienced in your life. See if you can pinpoint the significant past experiences that may currently be hindering your ability to feel good about yourself today.

_____

_____

_____

_____

2. Have you effectively worked through each experience and emotion? Please jot down some thoughts here to start the process of working through those emotions.

_____
_____
_____
_____

3. Which experiences continue to trouble you, and what steps have you taken to resolve the issues related to those experiences?

_____
_____
_____
_____

4. How do you think your unresolved issues related to these experiences and emotions might affect your current/future mate in an intimate relationship?

_____
_____
_____
_____

5. What actions are you willing to take to ensure your unresolved issues do not interfere with your happiness?

_____
_____
_____
_____

6. Please give careful consideration to the aforementioned questions. If you find that you cannot resolve your issues on your own, it is highly recommended that you consider seeking assistance from other sources. Some viable sources of assistance include, but are not limited to learning more about your family history, spiritual guidance, reading materials, group counseling sessions, and speaking to a trained mental health professional. Remember, your happiness is your responsibility.

We all have issues from our past. It is up to you not to bring your issues into your future. Those issues will handicap your ability to be happy with yourself in a new relationship. Your unhappiness with yourself will stifle your ability to maintain a happy and healthy relationship with your mates.

How is your self-esteem and your self-awareness? Having good self-esteem and good self-awareness are essential elements required to developing and sustaining good feelings about you.

To know yourself will facilitate your ability to attract people into your life who feel good about themselves as well. Please answer the questions listed below. See where you stand with yourself.

1. How do you see yourself at work with your peers?

_____

_____

2. How do you see yourself with family members?

_____

_____

3. How do you see yourself in social situations?

_____

_____

4. How do others see you?

_____

_____

5. How do you feel about yourself?

_____

_____

6. Do you love yourself?

_____

_____

7. If not, why not?

_____

_____

Learning to love yourself is one of the best self-help lessons you will experience.

In order to build your self-esteem, you have to discover all of the good things that make you special. Believe in what you discover about you. That will help you create a good feeling about who you are. This will generate self-confidence and boost your self-esteem.

Remember, to build anything good starts from the inside out. You can have a pretty face, beautiful long curly hair, and pearly white teeth, but if you do not feel good about yourself, your beautiful external features will not make you happy.

 As human beings, we all come in different colors, shapes, and sizes. Some of us are tall, some of us are short, some of us are chunky, and some of us are petite. One thing that we have in common is that we are all God's children. We all are born with special God-given talents and abilities. If I may suggest, try to discover another aspect of your beauty by realizing what gift God gave you. Then go on to be what you were born to be. Doing what you were born to do can lead to a much more fulfilled life.

Self-awareness

1. Who are you?

_____

_____

_____

2. Do you know anything about your basic family tree?

_____

_____

_____

3. What are your most important values in life?

_____

_____

_____

4. What tends to cause you emotional turmoil?

_____

_____

_____

5. What are your strengths and what are your weaknesses?

_____

_____

_____

If you lack self-awareness, explore your past with family members, medical records, family photo albums, and visit the place where you were born.

You can also explore websites that assist people with self-awareness concerns, i.e., ancestry.com. Improved self-awareness will help to improve your self-esteem and your self-love.

 To know yourself and where you come from can fill a big void in your life. Even if what you find out about your family background is not positive, it is better to know rather than wonder why things are so bad with your family life. Sometimes the bad things about your family can inspire you to do great things for your life and your family.

Learn to Let Go

Working through issues from your past relationships is vital to forming a healthy intimate relationship with someone else in the future.

Do you find yourself reflecting on your previous relationships? Do you sometimes feel pain when you think about a previous relationship?

If so, you may not have allowed yourself to experience closure. When you do not get proper closure, you may carry your heartfelt negative emotions with you into your new relationships. Your behavior regarding this lack of closure may have a negative impact on your new mate.

Below, there are five questions listed to assist you with the process of working through your issues regarding your past relationships. This is not something that will happen overnight. It is a process that will require you to come to terms with the reality that those relationships are over.

There probably will not be a second chance to be with that person again. In addition, it will be a challenge to understand that closure begins and ends with you. You may not always be able to rely on the other person to answer questions or to give you explanations regarding their actions. Therefore, whether or not you have the answers, you must learn to free yourself from memories that contribute to your unhappiness regarding your past relationships. You simply have to let go!

1.   What precludes you from finding closure in your past relationships?

_____

_____

_____

2.   Can you overcome those issues?

_____

_____

_____

3. What steps will you take to ensure that you successfully work through issues from your past relationships to bring some positive closure to those issues?

_____

_____

_____

4. What lessons have you learned from your previous relationships?

_____

_____

_____

5. How can you use those lessons to ensure that you do not repeat the same behavior regarding your issues with finding closure?

_____

_____

_____

Letting go can be hard to do especially if you hold on to something that is gone forever. When you allow yourself to look forward, you will allow yourself to experience the joy of your future.

It is quite simple. You have two options.

One, you can remain stuck in the memory of what causes you pain and holds your life back.

Or two, you can move on and enjoy what your future has in store for you. Stop trying to hurt your ex-mate. You indirectly hurt yourself in the process.

How to Handle Being Rejected

One of the risks of engaging in relationships is that at some point, the relationship may end and you may be rejected. Rejection could be defined as another person refuses to continue their relationship with you. Or, your spouse may decide to divorce you.

There is no doubt being rejected can be a blow to a person's ego. Such a blow could lead to emotional turbulence—anger, sadness, depression, and despair. Or if you remain positive about being rejected, it could be like hitting a speed bump before you start a new chapter in your life.

However, too often, for many of us, rejection may lead to emotional challenges, which prolong the intensity of the rejection. This perspective of rejection may keep your life in limbo.

Unless you are a robot, you will experience an emotional reaction to being rejected. Rejection can hurt, and depending on how you are rejected and the reason for being rejected, that will determine how long you will allow yourself to experience the pain of rejection.

Essentially, how you deal with rejection depends on your view of your past experiences. In addition, it will include your understanding of rejection and how you see yourself.

Please know that everybody who goes through life will face rejection in one way or another.

Everyday people are rejected by family members, lovers, employers, and friends. As much as it may hurt, rejection is a regular part of everyday life. Therefore, it would behoove you to not allow yourself to be derailed into extended periods of self-pity with negative emotions.

Remember, you still have a life to live, love to give, and love to receive.

It is a total waste of your time to focus on the person who rejected you. It would be more productive to realize it is about you and not the person who is out of your life. Keep the focus on yourself. You cannot change the person who rejected you. But you can change your behavior. You can change by focusing on you. Be cognizant of your thoughts and actions in the midst of being rejected.

For instance, are you thinking that you are no good because somebody declared they no longer want you in their life? Are you consumed with anger and thoughts of getting back at somebody? Do you spend countless hours devising plans to hurt the person who rejected you?

All of the above are counterproductive activities and will only intensify your feelings of rejection.

Below are five things you can do when you are faced with rejection.

1. Be real with yourself.

    No matter how hard you try, you cannot hide from yourself. Try to look at how being rejected has affected you. More specifically, determine what emotion is the rejection stimulating within you.

    Most of us try to hide from our real feelings. We tend to cover up our real emotions. We act like we are not being affected by what we feel. Then we act out in an angry manner.

    You may feel anger, but try to determine what emotion is beneath your anger. Admit to yourself if you are feeling sad because you were rejected. Talk to a close friend or mental health professional about your real feelings, if you have been hurt by being rejected. If you hide from your real feelings, you will only complicate the issues, which may lead to other problems.

2. Deal with your feelings.

    We often run from our feelings. We should sit with our feelings so we can actually experience our feelings.

    When you sit with your feelings, and allow yourself to feel that specific emotion, you have a chance to take control of your feelings. Then you can determine what you want to do with those emotions.

3. See your rejection as a learning opportunity.

    Being rejected could be one of the best learning opportunities you can experience. Pay attention and try to learn from that experience. If you are rejected by a significant other, do not blame the other person. You may not get much out of that process.

However, if you think about what you could have done differently, you may be on to something. Rejection can be a great time for self-reflection. This will give you a chance to take a look at how you may have contributed to being rejected.

If the truth be told, we all participate in some way or another in every rejection we experience in our lives. If you can determine how you contributed to being rejected, the rejection can serve as a valuable learning experience to prevent future rejection.

4.   Explore your childhood upbringing.

We all have been rejected at some point as a child. If you were ridiculed and judged when you were rejected as a child, as an adult, you may see rejection as humiliating and shameful.

However, if you were taught that rejection is a part of everyday life, as an adult you may not be troubled when you face rejection. What messages did you receive as a child when you were faced with rejection?

We tend to act out as adults based on the messages we learned as children. The good news is you can reprogram your messages. Then you can replace these messages with healthy productive messages.

For example, you can allow yourself to understand and accept that rejection is a part of life. And more importantly, you can handle rejection.

5.   Allow yourself to experience personal growth.

What would happen if you were never rejected? Would you grow as a human being? Do you need to grow?

If everyone said yes to you, then you would not need to change anything. You would not have to learn anything. That would lead to a boring life. Being rejected and criticized, in most cases, is an opportunity for you to grow. Resisting or hiding from rejection is an exercise in futility.

Learning from rejection can be fruitful and lead to personal growth. Take the time now to see what lesson you learned from being rejected.

What did you learn about yourself? What commitment can you make to yourself in future endeavors as a result of the lessons you learned from being rejected?

What to do when you are filled

with Anger and Bitterness

Do you spend an inordinate amount of time thinking about things like: how you were mistreated, mislead, offended, or rejected? Are you frequently devising schemes to get back at another person? Does your blood boil when you think about what somebody did or said to you?

If so, you may be covering up deep rooted feelings of anger, bitterness, and an assortment of emotions combined with bad experiences.

Please know that an unfortunate fact of life is that most people will one way or another be wronged by a close friend or family member. When you cross that bridge, if you are not careful, your anger and/or bitterness can destroy a great portion of your life.

It does not matter if you are right or wrong in a particular conflict with another person. If you hold resentment that leads to anger or bitterness toward the other person, then you do more damage to yourself.

In addition, if you prolong your anger and bitterness toward another person, your behavior would be considered highly abnormal. From a mental health perspective, such behavior could be diagnosed as insanity.

When you spend more time focusing on exacting revenge on another person versus enhancing your own life, you lose touch with reality. It is very important that you redirect your focus back to your own life. You must do this as soon as possible.

If you find that you cannot come to terms with the issues at hand, then consulting with a mental health professional would be warranted. Prolonged anger or bitterness is an emotion that suggests you have turned your emotions inward. That is a prescription for self-neglect and destruction.

If you do not have the resources to utilize the services of a professional, I would strongly recommend that you try to deal with your emotions head on. You must deal with your feelings by experiencing them. You can cry, you can talk, you can learn, you can let go, and you can forgive the other person.

For the record, when you forgive a person, you forgive them for your well being. Forgiveness has more to do with you than it does with letting the other person off the hook. To forgive is to free yourself from that person, that experience and hopefully from the memories related to your anger and bitterness.

The more anger or bitterness you feel, the further you move away from being your true self. It is imperative that you begin to realize that you spend too much time blaming the other person. Instead, you have to use your time doing a self-examination of your own behavior. That is the first step toward dissipating your anger and/or bitterness.

If you refuse to look at yourself, then you may have already evolved into a state of insanity. Only an insane person would spend their life consumed with anger and bitterness. You should be pursuing peace in your life.

Please let me suggest some remedies for you to overcome the anger and/or bitterness that may be overwhelming you at this time.

First, you have to look at your relationship with yourself. You cannot be good with anyone if you are not good to yourself. As a matter of fact, your personal, professional, and social relationships will be adversely impacted when you have a bad relationship with yourself. Therefore, some work is required for you to improve your relationship with yourself.

Second, the key to overcoming anger and bitterness is to look at the factors surrounding these emotions. Below, I have provided some additional steps with more detail for you to begin the process of moving past your anger or bitterness.

Step One: Examine your motivation for being angry and bitter.

Dealing with your inner self also suggests that you examine why you would want to experience and project feelings of anger and bitterness. What is your motivation for feeling bitter? Are you trying to get back at the other person? Do you want someone else to feel the pain, anger and distress you are experiencing? Do you allow yourself to dwell on what you think is fair and unfair?

Think about this. What is "Fair" about some people being born into prosperous families living a long time with more money than they can spend? While on the other hand, some people are born into poverty and die young after living a life filled with suffering.

Unfairness is all around us. We are surrounded by it every day and everywhere we go. It happens at work. It happens in the supermarket. It happens between brothers and sisters. It happens in criminal court cases. Unfairness happened for hundreds of years during slavery.

I recommend you abandon the thought of thinking everything in life should be based on fairness. We all have to accept the reality that some things in life are not fair. Some relationships and friendships do not last forever. Some people are more selfish than others. Some people are not into long-term mutuality. Some employers do not care about all of their employees. Some family members make mistakes.

Through it all, we have to accept the reality that all things in life are just not fair. There is no more or less to it. You can remain bitter, spiteful and angry forever. That behavior will not bring about any of the changes you might be looking for regarding your issues. And you will certainly stifle your ability to experience any peace in your life.

Please take some time to list your thoughts below as to why you are angry and bitter.

_____

_____

_____

_____

Step Two: Explore the underlying factors of your anger and bitterness.

To deal with your inner world implores you to explore the underlying factors regarding your anger and bitterness. Anger sometimes arises when a person feels a sense of helplessness. Or that they may be losing control of a situation.

Why are you feeling angry and bitter?

Take some time to think about it. When you do, please know that underneath feelings of anger and bitterness lies a deeper feeling, such as hurt and fear.

Admitting to being hurt or fearful is not a sign of weakness. In fact, it represents a sign of inner strength which can lead you into a better understanding of the issue you are experiencing.

When you get in touch with your pain and fear, what images, thoughts, and underlying issues are associated with them?

I suggest you write out your thoughts and feelings. Keep writing until you can determine the answers to what issue lies beneath your bitterness and anger. Every emotion we experience is connected to a thought. There is a cognitive representation of a person or a situation. When you ascertain what the underlying thoughts are, challenge your thought process to pin point the issues related to your thoughts. For instance, the underlying thought is that a person is mean because they chose to be with somebody else instead of you.

Think about that for a moment. When we examine some of our thoughts, we may find that some of our thoughts are unrealistic and perhaps unfair. Do you think it is realistic or fair for a person to stay with you when that person is not interested in you? Would you want to be with a person if you did not have the same romantic feelings for them as they have for you?

Quite often, when we examine our thoughts that lie beneath feelings of anger and bitterness, we may find our thoughts to be unfair and unreasonable. This awareness can help you to make better decisions for yourself. You may be able to think differently and more reasonably, which may release you from the feelings of anger and bitterness.

What is really causing you to feel anger and/or bitterness?

_____

_____

_____

_____

Step Three: Examine your underlying expectations.

I would like to also suggest that you examine your underlying expectations. Unfulfilled expectations can lead to anger and bitterness. What are your expectations for yourself and others in this situation? Are you expecting more than is realistic for this person in this particular situation?

157

Take a moment to examine your underlying expectations about what you need to be happy, and your needs to live a life filled with peace. Examine your expectations from others. It could be that you have higher standards for relationships than others. Perhaps you expect others to abide by your standards, but you may not have communicated those standards. Your standards may be right, however, those are your expectations for others, which are not their standards.

We have to keep in mind that people are who they are. No matter how much anger or bitterness you display, people decide who they want to be, and some people may never change. Moreover, anger and bitterness does not help you accept people for who they are, and it may not cause other people to change.

Let go of thinking that life should be fair. Let go of unrealistic expectations of others or events. You are not hurting anyone except for yourself. The pain you inflict upon yourself crosses over into many areas of your life physically, mentally, spiritually, and emotionally.

You must come to terms with the fact that your endeavor to be angry and bitter is an exercise in futility. Release yourself from the feelings of anger and bitterness. Work toward achieving peace and harmony in your life every day.

What are your underlying expectations?

_____

_____

_____

_____

Step Four: Let go and forgive.

Decide to forgive and be happy. Forgiving is not forgetting. It is remembering, learning, and letting go.

One of the keys to forgiveness is to work to see the situation from the other person's point of view. You do not have to agree with their perspective. You can endeavor to understand why they did or said how they felt according to their reality.

When we move toward understanding the other person's point of view, we will see that we all have hang-ups, struggles, and misconceptions. None of us are perfect. We all make mistakes. And we can decide to forgive. You forgive to let go in an effort to find peace and happiness.

Just as we decide to be angry and bitter, happiness is a choice we make for ourselves. You can decide to be happy or bitter. What emotions do you really want to project into your life? Joy? Peace? Love? Happiness? Anger? Bitterness? It is your life and your choice. You decide!

I would like to thank Dr. Kenneth B. Ballard, Professional Clinical Counselor, for contributing, creating, and developing all of the aforementioned exercises. These instruments were developed to address the emotional health needs of people who may be either unhappy with the result of their special relationships, or for the people on the receiving end of the anger and bitterness spewed upon them by an ex-mate.

Let Go of the Fight to be Right

If you are on the receiving end of the anger and bitterness of your ex-mate, at some point you may realize the fight may never end. The cost of freedom sometimes comes with a hefty price tag.

In this book, I told you about a father who gave up his rights due to the tremendous stress he experienced in the fight for his daughter.

His stress began to have an adverse impact on his health. Do not let that be your story. There are some good things that exist in your situation. You just have to look for the good and then go forward.

Below, you will see my suggestions for steps you can take to free yourself from the fight to be right.

1. Let go of the bad memories regarding the fights with your ex-mate.
2. Do not try to get even. Work toward getting some peace of mind.
3. Do not spend another dime to fight in family court. I have lost every one of my approximately twenty battles in family court. How many battles with your ex-mate have you won?
4. Everybody I know told me my daughter would come back to me. She came back two months after a judge took my overnight parenting time away. I spend more overnight time with her now than I did when I had a court order.

5. After you have prayed and cried, cried and prayed, and cried some more, if you have done all you can do, just leave it alone!
6. Let go and let God.
7. Live in the now. Take an assessment of your life. Realize the blessing that you are alive and well. Thank God for your good health, the health of your loved ones, your job, and all of the other things you may take for granted.
8. Stop crying about the injustices you received in family court. You will only perpetuate your pain and suffering.
9. Pray and meditate.
10. Do not be discouraged; always be encouraged.
11. Pursue your dreams.
12. Join a Fathers Rights Support Group.
13. Take better care of yourself: Do You!
14. Seek counseling from a therapist.
15. You can do something for yourself other than feel bad about the things you cannot control regarding your ex-mate and her family court system.

As you leave the Let-Go Lab, we hope you are in a better place mentally, emotionally, and spiritually before you visited this lab. Dr. Ballard and I want you to know that this is a place you can visit more than once. You can utilize these exercises over and over again.

However, if you find that these materials are not meeting your needs, please reach out to a mental health professional for your specific issues.

If you worked through these exercises, we commend you for your courage. It takes a person who is ready for change to start the process of striving toward improved emotional health. We built this lab to give you a vehicle to start the process to transform your mind, body, and soul. It may not happen overnight. It will happen if you start the process with an open mind and work through your issues on a daily basis.

Thank you for selecting this book to read. I hope that it heightened your awareness regarding the adverse impact of using children as pawns.

In addition, I hope that this book has encouraged you to handle your affairs with your ex-mate in a more positive fashion, which equates to what the judges say in family court, "My decision is based on what is in the best interest of the child."

May God bless you each and every day of your life. Make every day a good day for you.

In conclusion, my hope is that the information and stories provided in this book will transform your behavior regarding the way you may treat your ex-mate in your fight to spend time with your children.

We, as ex-mates, must work together to develop the emotional health of our children to build them up to survive in a world full of people who cannot wait to exploit their emotional weaknesses.

It is time to stop fighting with each other. Can we take the focus off us and focus on our children? We need to provide our children with the full armor of our love so that no weapon formed against them shall prosper!

Addendum

I dare not venture to minimize the miracle of a mother carrying a baby for nine months through morning sickness, fatigue, food cravings, weight gain, gestational diabetes, and the unspeakable pain of labour before the birth of a child.

However, mothers and judges should be mindful that none of this pain and joy along with the miracle of child birth would be possible without the healthy seaman provided by the father.

At this point, I believe the case has been made for the existence and significance of the father in the lives of his children. However, when will the courts render equal justice to support the enforcement of fathers parental rights? We need a family court system that renders win-win resolutions for both mothers and fathers to resolve their issues.

My hope is that this book serves as an instrument of enlightenment to raise peoples awareness regarding these very important subjects and issues. We need a family court system that promotes the well being of families after the break up of their relationships. And hopefully through attrition we can get rid of judges who are in the business of promoting and supporting the behavior of vindictive mothers, denying justice to loving fathers, and issuing court orders that are not in the best interest of our children!

The article below is a great description of the catastrophic current status of the bad laws and decisions that take place every day in our family court system throughout the United States. Please read this powerful article regarding our family court system that totally disregards the rights and dignity of good, law-abiding fathers.

"Gender Bias in Our Family Court System"

Our legal pendulum swings to yet another extreme. Gender bias runs rampant in our family court system. In the 1960's women fought hard to get laws passed to protect women against domestic violence. It took many painful years for our legal system to recognize women as victims of domestic violence. Domestic violence, stalking, and sexual harassment laws were passed and enforced to protect "true victims." Many women lived through domestic violence; many died. Some went to jail for homicide; some were later pardoned. We, as women, finally got society to recognize violence against women.

Shame on all those women of the 1990's who now use these laws to their advantage in family courts to bring men to their knees; and to erase fathers from the lives of their children! False allegations by women of child abuse, domestic violence, and stalking are almost never questioned by judges for fear of being politically incorrect. Women who feel justified in punishing men use these false charges indiscriminately. Children are forgotten and have become our newest victims with full cooperation from our Family Court system. Children need fathers too.

Women have become educated in the ways of our legal system. A new study purports women are filing 70% of divorces today. *The First person to file usually wins.* The unfortunate person against whom false allegations are charged must prove their innocence while a plaintiff proves nothing. As a paralegal and a woman, I am no longer proud of those of female gender who abuse our legal system.

An innocent father involved in a nasty contested divorce from a woman who vows vengeance is helpless in Family Court. Important child support laws enacted are now strictly and sometimes unfairly enforced. There are stories of fathers who lost their jobs from downsizing and/or circumstances beyond their control. When the mother of his children insists on back child support, he is thrown into jail. Child support is based on his "earning ability." Debtor's prison has become our most recent politically correct means to control men. Here again, our Family Courts condone whatever women allege, accuse, and dictate to control men.

Should a husband make the mistake of remarrying, further angering his ex-wife, a second wife's income is used as "a way to show ability to pay." The mother of their children, on the other hand, can marry another man. The "other man's" income is never used to lower child support. Court's rationale—"they are not his children, not his responsibility." Since when did a mother bear no responsibility for her children?

Today's women are earning more, and are becoming a majority in our workforce. The stay at home mom of the 50's rarely exists today. I know of a man who ended up paying so much child support (plus child expenses) he had to move back home with his parents. Yet his ex-wife earned more than he did.

False allegations of child abuse by a vengeful ex-wife devastates not only children, but fathers. The wife files first to take advantage of all laws passed to protect true victims of abuse and violence. The wife charges everything from domestic violence to stalking to child abuse. Courts almost always believe a woman over a man today. I know of a man who was falsely accused of child sexual abuse. By the time he was found innocent, he lost his job, his reputation, and everything he owned. Recent statistics do show women are becoming our primary child abusers, and yes, even killers of our children. Yet our Family Courts consistently believe, "the mother always makes the best parent."

Some mothers today emotionally blackmail and intimidate their children into fabricating abuse by their father. I know a man who fought two years to get custody of his son from a proven mentally ill mother who abused their son. Each time the court insisted "the mother is the best parent."

A large number of children are ordered to see a child psychologist when divorce is filed. Counselors and psychologists are encouraged by our system to give bad reports against a father. Fathers are automatically presumed capable of abuse before any mother. Mothers are intentionally denying visitation to loving, child support paying fathers, who then spend money and time in court trying to get visitation enforced. I know a man who hasn't seen his son in 14 years, but religiously pays his child support. He stopped pursuing visitation in court when the mother threatened to harm the son. Is this fair? Why is there no press on intentional denial of visitation"? One of the saddest true stories I know of is a little nine year old boy who was put in a mental institution by his mother until he stopped saying, "I want to see my daddy." There are too many stories of children committing suicide. I personally know of a woman who kept her teenage son up night after night crying about her divorce, repeatedly telling him "children ruin marriages." Her son turned to drinking, drugs, and dropped out of college. Divorce is a reality. It is currently a billion dollar a year business. Contested divorce is guerilla warfare whether people want to acknowledge it or not. Everyone wants fuzzy warm answers to harsh reality. There are none unless we all recognize the gender bias against males perpetrated in Family Court today, and the undeniable damage it does to our children.

Years ago women had a disadvantage in our domestic courts. Now they can feel quite happy knowing most women win. They can manipulate child support into "backdoor alimony," deprive their children of their fathers, and ruin their husband. Truth no longer exists in our legal system.

Yes we have come a long way. Women can be proud of the laws they fought hard for 30+ years ago. I am personally grateful for these laws. Let us not blaspheme those women who died for the very laws that many women are abusing today.

We must stop abusing these laws, or one day our legal pendulum will swing back and our true victims will not be believed again. You think you are beating men? You are beating yourself; destroying your children; and making the racketeers in our legal system rich. You are creating a generation of children who think love is conditional and possessive; who learn that violence by proxy and misuse of the law will make you a winner.

I will never be associated with any "feminist" movement which advocates false allegations, destroying children, and eliminating good fathers. Let's remember that it is children, not women, who are the real victims of the gender bias in our family courts. [5]

This article speaks directly to my own experience in the family court system. Based on my experience with the aforementioned issues noted in this article, I was inspired to write this book. And, I hope that this book will not only make a difference in your life and your dealings with any ex-mates and children, but also I hope you share this book with your family and friends to educate them about the horrors of Access Denied!

5   5. Harbour, Pearle. Gender Bias in Our Family Court System. fathermag.com. 2010-04-11. URL:http://www.fathermag.com/808/GenderBias.shtml. Accessed: 2010-04-11. (*Archived by WebCite® at http://www.webcitation.org/5ourepd6m*)